21 PSALMS

FOR THE 21st CENTURY

21 PSALMS

FOR THE 21st CENTURY

Process Meditations

Marjorie Hewitt Suchocki

WITH CONTEMPORARY PSALMS BY
Blair Gilmer Meeks

PROCESS
CENTURY
PRESS
ANOKA, MINNESOTA 2023

Process Century Press
RiverHouse LLC
802 River Lane
Anoka, MN 55303

Process Century Press books are published in association with the International Process Network.

Cover: Susanna Mennicke

VOLUME V
FAITH IN PROCESS SERIES
JEANYNE B. SLETTOM, GENERAL EDITOR
ISBN 978-1-940447-61-2
Printed in the United States of America

Alfred North Whitehead's process philosophy develops and explores the concept that all existence is necessarily relational. Nothing is isolated: all things are interconnected. Such theories are now commonplace in many of the sciences, but they are also deeply resonant with religious and theological thought. Perhaps the most profound religious expression of process thinking is the necessarily interrelational nature of all things, not only to one another, but also and centrally to God. Internally and externally, we exist in and through relationships. Many forms of process theologies have been developed in the decades since relational thinking deepened our understanding of reality.

Process Century Press has published a number of works dealing with relational theology. But theoretical work has not been the only mode of working with the relational structure of all existence—to the contrary, many practical implications have also affected personal and communal forms of religion. In this Faith in Process series, the Press looks to contemporary resources that enhance religious life, both personally and communally. It may well be that there is no greater need for such works than our present time. Given the flux in the contemporary world—the merging of politics and faith, renewed questions about who "qualfiies" to lead religious activities, tensions between freedom and responsibility, the scope of freedom for women and their own bodies, issues of migration, continuing racism—there are issues enough! Relational forms of thinking are needed now more than ever. And because we are indeed relational, interwoven with one another at our deepest levels, it may even be possible that works exploring and promoting our relationships to one another and to God may be part and parcel of our healing.

Marjorie Hewitt Suchocki

Table of Contents

⌒ 1ST MEDITATION ⌒

PSALM 137

By the Waters of Babylon

Read Psalm 137

ACERTAIN AMOUNT of underlying dread accompanied us during those first days of the pandemic. We hardly knew what to expect, save that a strange new disease threatened all of us—and we soon realized that the "all" was the whole world. We were ALL so vulnerable, and the dread deepened.

To deal with it, I decided on a spiritual discipline of reading a psalm each night—and once I reached Psalm 150, I'd start in all over again with Psalm 1. And because I had a small leather-bound 1929 prayer book that includes the Psalms, I kept that by my bed and used its King James version for my nightly Psalm. The archaic nature of that KJV somehow seemed comforting and stable, providing a way to address this very new thing in our world. And the Psalms were indeed comforting—I'll never forget the relief I felt when I read Psalm 91:10: "There shall no evil happen to thee, neither shall any plague come nigh thy dwelling!" It didn't matter that it was addressed millennia ago to a people far away; it was a comfort! And in addition to Psalm 91, there are so many other psalms of joy, beauty, and delight!

But not all my reading in the Psalms was a comfort. In fact, reading one after the other became clearly troublesome, for again and again I would read wishes that evil would befall the psalmist's enemies. Cumulatively these hard psalms bore upon my soul, with Psalm 137 being particularly problematic.

I was familiar with the first part of this psalm—how could I not be? Its plaintive and sublime lament had been woven into a lovely melody, sung as a round by high school youth groups. Here it is in the King James version:

> By the waters of Babylon we sat down and wept, when we remembered thee, O Zion. As for our harps, we hanged them up upon the trees that are therein, for they that led us away captive required of us a song, and melody in our heaviness: "Sing us one of the songs of Zion!" How shall we sing the Lord's song in a strange land? If I forget thee, O Jerusalem, let my right hand forget her cunning; if I do not remember thee, let my tongue cleave to the roof of my mouth, yea if I prefer not Jerusalem above my chief joy!

My heart heavy with feeling for the captives, I then read the final three verses:

> Remember the children of Edom, O Lord, in the day of Jerusalem, how they said, "Down with it! Down with it even to the ground!" O daughter of Babylon, wasted with

misery, yea: happy shall he be that rewardeth thee as thou
has treated us. Blessed shall he be that taketh thy children,
and throws them against the stones.

The New Revised Version of 1989 makes it even more stark: "Happy
shall they be who pay you back what you have done to us! Happy
shall they be who take your little ones and dash them against the
rock!"

How can this be holy scripture? How can it be that the tragedy
of the lament be capped with an equal or worse tragedy for citizens
of the conquering nation? And the cumulative effect of the many
imprecations within so many psalms began to work upon me.

With regard to Psalm 137, there is a sense in which one can
understand it. Chapters in the prophets Obadiah and Ezekiel detail
the awful, wanton killing of inhabitants that victors inflicted upon
defeated enemies, and in II Kings 8:12, the prophet Elisha fore-
sees what the future king of Aram will do to the people of Israel:
"you will set their fortresses on fire, you will kill their young men
with the sword, dash in pieces their little ones, and rip up their
pregnant women." Such viciousness ensured that no generation
would be left behind to rise up seeking vengeance. Also, Psalm
137 reflected the pain of the first generation of captives taken into
Babylonian exile, because they remembered Jerusalem, whereas
those born in captivity would only have heard of Jerusalem, not
seen or remembered it.

These first captives were on a forced march of 600 miles from
Jerusalem to Babylon. Even if their children had escaped the
slaughter, would they have left them behind? Would little ones
survive 600 miles of walking? How many died along the way?
Were parents even allowed to stop to bury their little bodies? Were
there burials every night? What did these captives endure in terms
of heartache? Their grief at the loss of their land was surpassed by

their grief over lost children, whether through the brutalities of slaughter or the brutalities of the long march. So one can imagine that their hatred of their captives was as strong as their love for their lost children, whether intentionally killed in warfare or lost during the long journey. And so the best they could do as they cried piteously beside strange waters was to wish upon their captives that which they had endured at their captives' hands. Does that make it right?

The Psalms, in particular, again and again and again praise the mercy and compassion of the God of Israel. And the laws established for the land of Israel, as we shall later see in the magnificence of Psalm 119, were to create a just and merciful society. How is it that one can express such dreadful vindictiveness to such a God?

And the answer, or so it seems to me, is that before God one is not to look for pious phrases or pretty poems: one is bound to utter honesty. And when the feelings with which one reckons are in fact contrary to religious teachings of mercy, one does not cover up the feelings; one expresses them before God, who already and always knows us as we are. God requires honesty of soul and life. And honesty in some circumstances can be dreadful, expressing a twistedness within ourselves to God, who is capable of receiving such laments and also capable of helping us to work through them.

Considering the plight of those ancient Israelites struggling in a land not their own, I began asking the further question concerning our own times in this twenty-first century—millennia later. This psalm details the misery of exile, of being forced to leave one's home and live a subservient lifestyle in a land far different from the homeland left behind. Are there not awful parallels in today's society? As for the divisions of one group taunting another, are the political divisions in our own society any less intense or vindictive than the attitude of Psalm 137? Whether for good or for ill we are inexorably connected with one another; the issue is not whether we respond, but how we respond. And so began this project of contemplating the whole variety of psalms, those that delight but also those that trouble us. For I am convinced that these long ago psalms have much to teach us in our twenty-first century world.

To that end, we shall consider selected psalms, and let the psalms lead us into "points to ponder" for how we live today. And following each psalm's discussion we will continue our work through prayers that are like contemporary psalms, written for us by Blair Gilmer Meeks—an author and editor who has taught classes in liturgical studies at Vanderbilt University. Study, contemplation, and prayer may go a long way in guiding us toward faithful living in this twenty-first century.

POINTS TO PONDER

Our first twenty-one years and more of this century have given us far too many parallels to the forced migration of those long ago Israelites. The parallels, to our sorrow, are worldwide as persons flee egregious civil wars in their homeland, or wars intentionally destroying the very means of life in an already poor land, or climate catastrophes such as rising sea levels, on the one hand, and desertification on the other, threatening food production and survival in places that had been safe homes for generations.

In America we experience mass migration attempts by persons fleeing intolerable cruelty, poverty, and hunger in their homelands. How do we whose families may have lived here for generations treat those who hope so deeply now for safety within our borders? Do we taunt them? Despise them? Blame them? Push them back? Or do we need them to replenish workers no longer available for particularly dangerous or monotonous work in our country? How do we treat contemporary migrants? We worship a God whose compassion and mercy is over us all. How can we begin to grow our own compassion and mercy to affect attitudes and actions toward migrants?

CONTEMPORARY PSALM/PRAYER

Loving God, you hear the cries of suffering people everywhere;
remember in your mercy those driven from their homelands.
Comfort and protect the refugees and exiles. Hear their
 prayers of longing.
Accept their anger and fear. Weep, O God, with those who
 weep.

Make your presence known to those who cannot sing songs
 of joy.
Remember all people who struggle at home in once familiar
landscapes, now made alien by conflict and Covid.
Give us courage to bring to you our sorrows and our rage.

We long for old comforts and pray for healing.
We pray for accountability and an end to brokenness.
Give us patience to wait for the vengeance that belongs to you.
Grant us grace to remember that our home is in you, O Lord.
You are our dwelling place now and forever.

— 2nd MEDITATION —

PSALM 29

A Symphony in a Psalm

Read Psalm 29

Sometimes you can almost hear a symphony inside a psalm, as if the words you read are indeed "music to your ears." Psalm 29, one of the most ancient psalms, is like that—and its symphony could be kin to Beethoven's Sixth, the Pastoral ... or perhaps it's Vivaldi's violin concerto of the seasons, expressing a storm in summertime. Read this psalm—and oh, can't you hear it? And isn't it sheerly a delight?

The introductory and concluding verses of the psalm are pro forma, ascribing glory to God. But in between this beginning and ending the orchestra takes over to describe the marvel of God as not only Lord of the Storm, but even, if one dare think it, as the Storm itself. Lightning flashes and horns blare; thunder crashes, and so do drums; wind blows and the strings soar. God is not only Lord of the storm, God *is* the storm! And the glory is almost unbearable.

We so enmesh God in our little human affairs—our little lives, our great plans: our intimacies and our anguishes, our comings, and our goings. And, of course, we pull God into our politics (odd, isn't it, how sure we can be about God's political preferences)! We implore and claim God's will for our international affairs. We send God into our battles to win our victories and decry our losses; indeed, we embroil God in all the iotas of our lives. And in many ways this is good—don't many of the psalms also do that in Israel's affairs? Of course, we deem that well and good. Isn't it how things are supposed to be?

But sometimes . . . sometimes. We come across something like Psalm 29. And it's as if God breaks free of our human preoccupation with ourselves, leaping into the freedom of a storm, rejoicing in its wildness, exulting in its roaring, glorying in its thunder. It's almost as if God simply takes a holiday from us and even frolics in the freedom of the storm—the freedom of God, who *is* the storm! And in God's wild temple, everything says "GLORY!" And just as we are almost beside ourselves with the wonder of what we are seeing, what we are hearing, what we are reading . . . the symphony, the concerto, slows down; the storm subsides . . . and there is simply quiet, radiant sunshine.

And yes, we come to the last verse, re-establishing that "the Lord sat as King at the flood; yes, the Lord sits as King forever." It's not the wild storm now, but back to business as usual. Now we can ask God, politely or perhaps desperately, to become involved, please, in our human affairs. "Give strength to your people . . . bless us with peace." We return to the prosaic.

But listen, listen! Don't you hear echoes of the music still? Or does it yet play, somewhere just beyond our hearing? Oh, yes! God of Glory! Praise God!

POINTS TO PONDER

The storm in the countryside and forests of Lebanon was one thing nearly three millennia ago. And even storms in the forests of Europe that inspired the poetic musicians of the eighteenth and nineteenth centuries were "tame" storms by twenty-first century standards. Today's storms break all records: storms of fire, raging across Siberia, Canada, the United States, Greece—storms of wind and water, bearing down on the Caribbean Islands, Mexico, the Gulf and Eastern coasts of America, cyclones battering the cities of Asia, destroying life in their paths. And there are ominous signs of horrific storms to come as the Gulf Stream, so important to the climate of Britain, Europe, and the Americas begins to waver and wobble, leaving its age-old life-giving paths in the Atlantic. We have reason enough to respect storms, for in Psalm 29 we even see God in a storm. But we are stewards of the Earth, are we not? And our lax stewardship is leading to lessening the age-old paths dictating weather patterns. How do we speak up for deeper, more responsible stewardship of the Earth? How do we in religious communities participate in lowering the carbons in our atmosphere? We may no longer be able to return to the climate even of the industrial age—but we might yet mitigate the damage we cause. How can we lessen our carbon footprint on this our God-given planet? How do we fulfill our responsibility to be people of God with the care of God's good Earth in our sometimes reckless hands?

OUR CONTEMPORARY PSALM/PRAYER

God our maker and mover,
you spoke to the prophet Elijah in the sound of silence,
but we confess that we too often ignore the stillness of your
voice.

Astonish us! Let us hear your thundering in the rushing wind,
the whirling oaks, the trees that bend and break, the swelling
    of the waves,
the wildfire's crackle and roar, the earthquake's shudder.
Shake us up and open our eyes to the majesty of your presence.
Strengthen us that we may reject the squandering of Earth's
    gifts.
Guide us to resist the neglect and carelessness that lead to
    disaster.
Empty us of complacency that we may be filled with love
    for your creation.
Surround us with your symphony of jubilation, your chorus
    of freedom.
Let us again shout: "Glory to the One who rules in holy
    splendor!"
"Praise to the One who blesses us with peace!" Amen.

— 3rd MEDITATION —

PSALM 68

A Father to the Fatherless

Read Psalm 68

THE COMPLEXITIES of Psalm 68 take us on a journey of memory, primarily depicting the movement of the Ark of the Covenant from Mt. Sinai to its enthronement on Mt. Zion in Jerusalem. The psalm culminates with a joyous depiction of the tribes of Israel accompanying the Ark as it goes up the slopes of Zion toward the temple: representatives of each tribe go beside the Ark, with singers, girls with tambourines, and finally the musicians following in their train. Celebration! The Ark comes home to Zion; Israel's God, YHWH, is enthroned in the temple.

Overall, this psalm, ascribed to David, recounts the wonders of Israel's history, focusing on the movement from Sinai to Zion, but also referencing the earlier journey from Egypt to Sinai. Sprinkled through the account are amazing tidbits of just what God is like. Yes, God is a God of valor, for how could that not be so given the eventual triumph of Israel? And yes, God is a God of nature, for God is Lord of the whole world, surely inhabiting more than simply temples—but also the mountains, the fields, the forests. There is nowhere where God cannot be found. But primarily the revelation of God through nature and temples is surpassed through covenant: God initiated and established a covenant with Israel, guaranteeing them God's steadfast love and faithfulness. The main wonder and depth of this covenant is not just mighty deeds of valor, but the very nature of the covenantal community, as it manifests compassion in its very structure. This nature of God's reign is captured in verses 5 and 6:

"Father of orphans and protector of widows is God in his holy habitation. God gives the desolate a home to live in; God leads out the prisoners to prosperity . . ." This is a recurring phrase throughout the Psalms, placed here in the context of history and worship. Consider the impact of such a persistent description of God in a patriarchal society such as Israel's. Think of the plight of those who, because of death, abandonment, or other form of loss, have no father. What of children who have neither family nor home? Too often the country was besieged by wars on every side, with many a father lost in battle. What of their now fatherless children? One would imagine there were unwed mothers in Israel; what of children born with no named father? What will be their lot in life? In a world where the status of the child depends upon the status of the child's father, the loss is double. destining such a child to be the lowest of the low, lacking standing and status.

Now consider the awesome power of the psalm: God is the father of the fatherless, and therefore it is the Lord God of heaven and Earth who conveys status to that child. How, then, is society to treat the fatherless? And the answer is, with respect and honor and care—the whole society now picks up the honor of tending a child of God.

God is also a "protector of widows," and once again the message is similar. A widow has no husband, no one to intercede for her, no one to provide for her—therefore she is vulnerable to exploitation and poverty, and who is to be her advocate? The psalm gives the answer: God. God is her protector. God will provide. God will protect. How, then, should the society worshiping God deal with the widow as well as the orphan? Surely it is the privilege and duty of the society at large to step in and care for the widow, as well as the orphan.

Do you see it? God is, in effect, the safety net for those without power or place, and the society that worships God picks up the mantle of care and provision.

But there is more: "God gives the desolate a home to live in." Oh, see now: how does this happen? And once again, the people who serve God are the mediators of God, the caregivers of God; they are those whose work it is to see to it that we have a society in which no one is left out, no one left to fend only for themselves, no one condemned to friendlessness and sorrow, no one without a home to live in.

Finally, God "leads out the prisoners to prosperity." Now there's a challenge, for our own society has seen to the very opposite: we have built more and more prisons—some in the heart of the harshest environments, such as the deserts in the southwestern states—and we have seen to the full occupancy of these houses of "correction" (or so we say). What agony! But the psalm says God wills that we shall lead these prisoners out. And not only out, but into prosperity. How in God's name are we to do that? Perhaps that's just it: in God's name. There are prisons throughout our country that focus on giving prisoners skills that they can use to sustain themselves in the larger society; aren't these like prisoners "led out into prosperity," if prosperity is the ability to earn one's

living and support a family? And there are colleges that, in col-
laboration with prisons, provide studies for inmates that can lead
to a four-year degree. Is that not also a way to release prisoners to
prosperity?

This psalm presents so many challenges—widows, orphans,
migrants, the homeless, and even prisoners. Isn't it too much?
Exactly what kind of a society does God expect us to be, anyhow?
The answer, says this psalm, is a society that cares for the
vulnerable, doing what it can to lessen that vulnerability. It is a
society that sees to equitable judgments for all, and not simply
for the well-to-do; a society that surrounds its individuals with
offers of care and friendship, and a society that looks to those
we call least—the locked up, the vagrant, the homeless—with
compassion and care.

To set these descriptions of God and God's people in the context of a psalm celebrating the movement of the Ark from Sinai to
Zion, and indeed, the people from Egypt through Sinai to Zion,
is to set them in the context of both history and of worship. The
heart of Israel's historical and religious journey, then, is marked by
learning to become a society that exercises compassion and care to
the most vulnerable of its people, and even toward strangers within
its gates. To be such a society is to be a people of God.

POINTS TO PONDER

The psalm lays out our agenda; we start with the most powerless
in our society. The structure of twenty-first century America is
not at all the structure of ancient Israel, and neither could it be
nor should it be. But just as that ancient society could name the
vulnerable among them—and go beyond that naming to claim
God's particular care for the vulnerable—so can we. Where would
we start? The question might better be, where should we stop?

Is there homelessness in our society? Hunger? Those wrongfully accused? Migrants? Crowded prisons? What about local laws that pile fee upon fees on prisoners who are released after paying for their crime through imprisonment? By piling on fees they have no way of paying, aren't we doing the exact opposite of "releasing them to prosperity"? And what about those in our society who cannot afford medical care? Try making a list of the vulnerable—if you dare! For the problem with such a list in light of this psalm is that God pulls all these persons into divine care. But before you sigh in relief, "Ah, good! God can take care of all that," look once again at the psalm. God assigns that care to the people of God. And we are God's people. We have work to do. How shall we carry it out?

CONTEMPORARY PSALM/PRAYER

God of majesty, you ride high upon the clouds,
but we know you as the protector of widows and orphans.
You make home for the desolate, provide for the hungry,
restore hope to prisoners, and attend to the children.
We are your people; strengthen us that we may give help in
your name.
Powerful God, empower us for the transforming of our
community.
Grant us grace to safeguard the vulnerable, sustain the weak,
and extend to all the fullness of life that comes from your
bounty.
You overcome those who rebel against your word,
and you scatter those who delight in war, who desire only
esteem and riches.
Let all nations and peoples stretch out their hands to you
for to you belongs escape from death; you bear us up every day.

Sing praises to your name, our awesome God who dwells
   with us.
Give thanks for all the works our God has done. Amen.

～ 4th MEDITATION ～

PSALM 42

Why Are You in Despair, O My Soul?

Read Psalm 42

THERE ARE so many psalms of delight we can hardly name them all. But if the psalms are to reflect life, the religious experience, or even just the human plight, they would not meet our spiritual condition if they never mention the despair into which our spirits can fall. We are emotional as well as intellectual beings, and both are deeply important—but we sometimes maintain the refrain, "it is well with my soul," over against spiritual or physical troubles that can overwhelm us. This is the case for the writer of the 42nd psalm.

The psalm proceeds in three stanzas, and the sense of despair pervades all three. The first stanza begins with the memorable image of a thirsty deer, frantically looking for a stream to assuage its thirst: "As the deer longs for flowing streams, so my soul longs for Thee, O God!" But even as the water eludes the thirsty deer, so it seems does God elude the God-thirsty soul. Plunged into despair, the psalmist can only look back longingly to a time when things were different, when God was so close that the psalmist could leap for joy. For there was a time when the psalmist led processions into the house of God, celebrating God's blessing—God's *presence*—in a time of festival. The memory is so strong—but all the more painful because its strength highlights the dreadful pain of God's absence now. Where, oh, where is God who is a "very present help in time of trouble," as some psalms assert? Where is God when all seems bleak? Where is God when all IS bleak? The psalmist breaks down in despair.

The second stanza raises the possibility of hope. Despair continues, but now rather than remembrance of a time of joy, of festival, of thanksgiving with and among the people of God, the psalmist remembers God as known of old. The remembrance is listed as a memory of things past; hope hasn't yet dared to raise the issue of God's continuance. Rather, the psalmist places God in the context of "the land of the Jordan," Israel. Is the psalmist no longer in Israel? Is this a psalmist now living in exile, fearful that God is present only in the land of Jordan? Is God but a tribal God, so that to be away from the land is to be totally away from God? Oh, God! What horror in such a fate! And despair deepens lest such an awful thing be true. "I remember thee from the land of Jordan, and of Hermon, from Mount Mizar," cries the psalmist. "Deep calls to deep at the thunder of your cataracts; all your waves and your billows have gone over me!" Is God even in the billows? If God is not confined to a sacred space such as the temple, then the shadow of hope begins to appear. Even in despair, the psalmist cries out in remembrance, "By day the Lord commands YHWH's steadfast love, and at night YHWH's song is with me . . ."

Stanza 3 takes the psalmist from the realm of memory to the terrors of the present. The memory of the festival has fled; the memory of God, powerful in nature, likewise; the present intrudes in all its awfulness. And despair tumbles from our psalmist's mouth again. God has forgotten him; his enemies oppress and revile him. It's as if all his bones are shattered, there is no strength left to rise up. And the taunting goes on, and on, and on: "Where is your God?" The question is a taunt, for no God is in evidence. At this point the psalmist's question seems rhetorical indeed: "Why are you cast down, O my soul? And why are you disquieted within me?"

And finally, here, at the very close of the psalm, the bitter triumph of hope even in the midst of despair re-emerges. Yes, the psalmist is in misery, enduring taunts, enduring a seemingly absent God. But: "Hope in God, for I shall again praise God"—and hear now the ringing triumph of the conclusion—". . . my help AND MY GOD!" God remains my God; there are times when I feel God's presence, and there are bleak times when I feel only an absence. NONETHELESS: whether in presence or in absence, God *is*. God's love is steadfast, even and perhaps especially in despair. Therefore, "Hope in God, for I shall yet praise God, my help and my God!" Trust triumphs.

POINTS TO PONDER

Thank God for psalms of lament and even despair, for if all the psalms had to give us were "happy thoughts for happy times," what good would the psalms be to us at all? We live in a time that knows of pandemics past, present, and future; of polarities threatening to pull our nation apart; where we, a nation of immigrants, seem to disparage those who beg to become immigrants, where we cannot even seem to trust each other, let alone trust immigrants. Who are we? Internationally, nations threaten nations, and even nuclear disaster emerges again as a present threat and danger. The world's troubles are every nation's troubles, for our planet is small, and we are irrevocably interconnected with one another. Do we sometimes despair of the way "things" are going? Do we ever ask, "but where is God, our "very present help in time of trouble"? Aren't we in trouble enough? Who are we, as a nation among nations, a people among peoples?

Perhaps in such a time as this we need to look again at this and other psalms of lament. Perhaps we need to use them to name our current despair, to use them to remember when times were different, to use them to ask the question of hope's reality. And perhaps in recognizing the pertinence of this psalm of despairing lament, we might begin to test out what it is to live as a people who hope in God anyhow—and act like it.

CONTEMPORARY PSALM/PRAYER

Living God, like the deer, searching for flowing streams,
we long to behold your face. Trembling, we ask, "Has God
   forgotten us?"
Turn us away from dread and despair;
help us remember that you never cease to be our God.
Give us courage when our belief in you is questioned,
when some fail to comprehend your boundless love and call
   us godless.
In times past we assembled for the holy meal
and found the joy of your presence in the gathered body of
   your people.
But now risk and fear keep us apart; we taste no holy bread,
   only tears.

Grant us grace to know your voice, to hear again your song
   in the night,
bringing calm assurance like a mother's lullaby.
We long for your living water and your peace to quiet our
   unease,
for you, O God, are our help and hope, our rock in a weary
   land.
May your steadfast love guide all our days
and bring us again to sing your praise. Amen.

── 5th MEDITATION ──

PSALM 23

I Will Fear No Evil

Read Psalm 23

THE BEAUTY of this psalm lies in its profound simplicity. Six short verses—yet within them lie edges of fear overtaken by deepest trust. Despair? No! Rather, the despair that is acknowledged deep within the soul is transformed into delight through God's sustaining care.

Ascribed to David, the 23rd psalm brims with trust in God no matter how hard the circumstances—and the circumstances could be very hard indeed. The book of 1st Samuel details much of the hardship of David's life prior to becoming king; he knew hunger in the wilderness as he hid in caves from a murderous and jealous king. And he certainly knew fear of death, not only in battle, but in narrow escapes from the king's plots against him. This psalm of confidence and joy rises from experiences of terror and loss; it is a psalm in which delight triumphs over despair.

So look at the movement of this psalm. David, who had once been a shepherd himself, now sees himself and all people as "sheep," with none other than the Lord's own Self as the Shepherd. From his own experience David knew the importance of "green pastures" and "still waters"; he knew the care it took to provide such sustenance for his sheep. "If," he might have thought, "I took such care of my sheep, how much more does God care for us?" In caring for us, the very Lord God restores our souls, enabling our restored selves to walk in paths of righteousness. And what are these "paths of righteousness"? Might we not dare to think that such paths are participating in God's work of caring? Of providing? Of restoring? We who follow this Shepherd of all shepherds—might we become "shepherds" ourselves? Surely this would be a path of righteousness, for God's sake.

Having been led in the way of trust, the psalmist now takes us to the heart of the psalm—the experience of walking through the valley of the shadow of death. David had done that. We have done that. Every human who has ever been has known this lonesome valley of shadows. And here is where trust rises yet again in triumph: even here in this valley, God is with us. We who live have sensed this valley, either through holding the hands of those we love during their passage into death, or perhaps also through our own deliverance of having been near death but miraculously returned to life. And all of us who draw from the biblical tradition will eventually live this psalm within our own souls, feeling its comfort as the precious words repeat themselves within our still living consciousness when we finally traverse this valley. There will be a strange peace in the journey, even despite the pain of letting go. We will be alone and yet not alone, for the Shepherd will be there, guiding us through in a fullness of love. Depths of trust and comfort will sustain us, and we will fear no evil.

But now, in the present, we emerge from this valley and find the psalmist has yet another triumph in store for us—one more delight in a situation otherwise boding fear and trembling. The first verses of this psalm touch upon the need for physical suste-nance—food, drink, a place to belong, and work to do—and the middle verses take us through the extremity of life in the valley of the shadow of death. But now . . . what is this? We are in fact in the presence of our enemies?

Again, reading the life of David in first and second Samuel is extremely instructive when it comes to understanding these psalms, for seemingly David was in constant trouble, surrounded by enemies, such that the only real friend he could count on was Jonathan, son of the king. And at the end of 1st Samuel, Jonathan has died. What would it be like, if those you have always counted on to sustain you emotionally can no longer do so, whether through distance, illness, or even death? With all your trusted "supports" removed, how could you handle it?

Like David. He has emerged from the valley of the shadow of death, he fears no evil. And there are the enemies. Wouldn't the David we are coming to know simply laugh? Ah, yes, and there is God preparing a table before him, in the presence of these very enemies. If God be with us and for us, who can really be against us? So, David eats and drinks in joy; God is with him. And in a precursor to David's becoming king, following the death of Saul, he knows his head will once again be "anointed with oil." He can remember himself as a lad, called from his work with the flocks, to meet this strange man who anointed him with oil. And David knows he will be anointed again, when he will be crowned king of Israel. So now, in the presence of his enemies? Shall he not laugh? He has come through the valley, he is fearless before enemies, and his cup indeed overflows. The Lord God is his Shepherd.

So finally, regardless of any and every trouble, regardless of each and every hardship, regardless! Goodness and mercy will always be deeper than any trouble, and goodness and mercy shall and will follow David all the days of his life. With God as his Shepherd, David can and does face anything. And so, with such a Shepherd, can we. And like David, we will dwell in the house of the Lord—forever. Amen!

POINTS TO PONDER

Usually we think in somewhat hierarchical terms with regard to "shepherding"—historically, Israel's kings took the title, even while acknowledging God as their ultimate shepherd. Thus, the king became the shepherd of the people of Israel. In Christian times, we have given the title of "pastor" and "pastoral leadership" to the ordained clergy, signifying that they are shepherds over us, their flock.

Who are today's God-anointed shepherds? Governments? World organizations? What about us? God leads us in green pastures, beside still waters, providing rest and also work, because the purpose of God's shepherding is so that we might freely walk paths of righteousness. How do we do that in this twenty-first century world, where the pastures are no longer green, the waters no longer safe? A twentieth-century German philosopher, Martin Heidegger, called humans "shepherds of being." If we ourselves, and not just our leaders, are called by God to be "shepherds," how do we obey that call? Imagine ways that we as ordinary people might actually walk in "paths of righteousness." Imagine being a shepherd of being in a world of creeping dangers and divisions and desperations. Imagine that God, our Ultimate Shepherd, commissions us all to the work of shepherding, despite the risks of lost profits, lost conveniences, and especially lost complacency! How would we do it? Can we do it? By God, it is possible! Let us figure out how it is possible, despite our foolish and useless divisions, to work together to develop the "how."

CONTEMPORARY PSALM/PRAYER

> God our shepherd, in this good, broad place we call home,
> where nevertheless death shadows us daily,
> lead us from despair to light.
> You have washed us in the still waters of baptism;
> you set your table for us and for all who call your name.
> You created us and called us to live in your image.
> Give us courage to be shepherds in your likeness,
> to care for our threatened planet and all who live here.
> Show us pastures made fertile by flocks as they feed,
> and green with rain that falls like your mercy from heaven.
> Cast out our fears and lead us to your living water.
> Gather us with all your people, even those who trouble us.
> Grant us grace to love our neighbor and find your peace.
> And so through all our days, trusting that your goodness
>   never fails,
> may we sing your praise and dwell with you forever. Amen.

— 6th MEDITATION —

PSALM 139

See if There Be any Hurtful Way in Me

Read Psalm 139

S URELY PSALM 139 is among the most beautiful passages in all scripture; it is a paean of praise to the omnipresent God who pervades the whole of existence—and therefore, also, ourselves. Reading Psalm 139 is like being a little child, wrapped in a feather quilt of delectable warmth, on a cold winter night. Safe . . . warm . . . loved. And when we close our eyes, it is with the sure expectation that when we wake, we will know God is yet with us, and has been, all through the long night, be it ever so dark.

The psalm begins with the delightful assurance that God knows us thoroughly—what we do, what we think, what we hope. And as if that weren't enough, God's knowledge of us is so deep and

true that God knows us better than we know ourselves—and such
knowledge is "too wonderful for me; it is high; I cannot attain it!"
Think of it. To be fully known, and yet to be accepted!

From this beginning, the psalmist exults in the fullness of
God's presence—there is literally NOWHERE we can go where
God is not. The psalmist plays with the notion: "shall I ascend to
heaven? . . . make my bed in Sheol? . . . take the wings of the morning
and dwell in the uttermost parts of the sea?" You can almost hear
the psalmist laughing in glorious delight and happiness.

> Even there thy hand shall lead me, and thy right hand
> shall hold me. If I say, "Let only darkness cover me, and
> the light about me be night—even the darkness is not
> dark to thee! The night is bright as the day, for darkness
> is as light with thee."

The power of the psalm is that we can practically hear that
ancient psalmist sighing in deep comfort and gladness, rejoicing
in the unfailing presence of the surrounding God. And if it were
true for that long-ago psalmist, it is also true for us, here, today. It
is indeed too high for us; we cannot comprehend it, yet we, like
the psalmist before us, exult in it.

The psalmist continues by imagining the time before "his" (alas,
probably not "her" given the customs of the times) birth—even
there, God was with us, knowing us, present to us.

And then our psalmist steps back, to reflect now not so much
on God, as on himself before God—and it is just here that we are
jolted from that warm comforter and thrown into the cold night.
Far from speculating concerning God's presence to all creation, the
psalmist draws back to focus on himself as opposed to the "wicked."

> O that thou would slay the wicked, O God, and that men
> of blood would depart from me, men who maliciously defy

thee who fit themselves up against thee for evil. Do I not hate them that hate thee, O Lord? And do I not loathe them that rise up against thee? I hate them with perfect hatred, I count them my enemies.

And then: "Search me, O God, and know my heart! Try me, and know my thoughts! And see if there be any wicked way in me, and lead me in the way everlasting."

As for us, we collapse, exhausted at the turn the psalm has taken, and praying that the last petition had some effect on the psalmist's self-righteous "perfect hatred" against those he deemed haters of God. Perhaps the psalmist knew persons whose wealth grew by intentionally defrauding the poor, or who despised immigrants, or who brazenly mocked God. Is it right for the psalmist to ask God to kill them? Or is it for the psalmist to determine who of his countrymen are or are not "haters of God"? And is it the psalmist who is to be held up as a standard, against whom all others are to be judged? And we who read this psalm—do we in our own day make ourselves the standard by whom the righteousness of others is to be judged?

The psalm itself pushes us away from such judgmentalism. There is no place where God is not; therefore, God is with those who think differently from us, those who worship differently, those who vote differently, those who evaluate social issues differently . . . God is with them. A hymn sings, "There's a wideness in God's mercy, like the wideness of the sea." Perhaps it is possible for us, through the strength God provides us, to see and love the wideness, and approach those who seem strange or wrong or different with openness and an outstretched hand. Perhaps—just perhaps?—there is more than one individual or people other than those like "us," who feels wrapped in a soft down quilt on a cold winter's night, covered by the loving and thoroughgoing presence of the omnipresent God.

POINTS TO PONDER

If we were honest enough, would we find in us a grim pleasure in the way some churches are torn apart between differing opinions as to whose sexuality is offensive to God? By so clearly defining those who disagree with us on the issue, don't we claim that we, not they, are aligned with the righteousness of God? Shall we split a church over it? Surely it has happened before, over a hundred years ago, when differences concerning race and slavery and who might worship with whom in the worship of an omnipresent God split more than one denomination thoroughly in two. Why not do it again, and tear the church apart in our self-righteousness?

It is so easy to direct our ire against those whose social or political views disagree with our own. If God loves and knows us, and we think thus and so, would it not be the case that those who think differently deserve our ire—or better yet, God's condemnation? Do we quickly take on the role of judge and jury, determining the just punishment of those with whom we disagree?

It is so that we are called to discernment over many things, But what we are surely not called to do is to set ourselves up as the standard by which those who differ from us are to be judged. How do we as a community discern the "wideness in God's mercy"?

CONTEMPORARY PSALM/PRAYER

God of hope, you are the light that drives away all shadows.
You know us altogether: you search our deepest thoughts
    and fears.
We praise you for never losing hope for us.
Gather our doubts and anxieties into the meaning you give
    our lives.
Comfort us, for you know our hurt; you know the "hosts of

evil round us."
Hear our anguished cries and embrace us with your perfect
   love.
Give us courage to fly on the wings of the morning,
knowing we will find you there, even beyond the boundaries
   of our comfort.
You, loving God, are the source of care beyond our knowing,
and you forgive beyond our ability to confess.
We cannot count the ways you come to us in every time
   and place,
nor comprehend the vastness of your thoughts.
Grant us grace to welcome your discerning presence that
   will not let us go.
Give us songs to praise you, for you have created us to be a
   fearful wonder,
intricate in variety, abounding in possibility, sustained by the
   wideness of your mercy.
Set us singing on our way to life in all its fulness, encompassed
   by your love. Amen.

— 7th MEDITATION —

PSALM 22

Why Hast Thou Forsaken Me?

Read Psalm 22

PSALM 22 is familiar to those who know the gospel accounts of Jesus' crucifixion, for the evangelists, writing more than forty, fifty, and even sixty or more years after events they had not witnessed, drew heavily from this psalm and also psalm 69:21 ("they gave me vinegar to drink") to describe what in their own minds seemed synonymous with what must have happened on that dreadful day. Psalm 22 begins with a lament of the direst sort: the agony of feeling abandoned by the God one has loved and served throughout life. In addition to the agonizing pain of body, there are also the taunts, mockery, and insults thrown at the suffering one by those choosing to witness and even celebrate the grimness of the awful event.

35

But then, suddenly, after 20 verses describing dreadful pain of body and soul, the psalm takes an enormous turn: God intervenes. Restoration! Resurrection! Joy! "Save me from the mouth of the lion" in verse 21 is followed by "you have rescued me! I will tell of your name to my brothers and sisters in the midst of the congregation . . . for YHWH did not hide YHWH's face from me, but heard when I cried . . . God did not despise or abhor the affliction of the afflicted; God . . . heard when I called!" After beginning with deepest physical and spiritual pain, this psalm ends with a shout of amazed triumph.

And neither do the gospel accounts leave us with desolation. To the contrary, throughout the gospel accounts we see Jesus joining us in our condition, experiencing hunger, weariness, persecution, abandonment—and finally experiencing wrenching pain of body and soul in the sense of abandonment on the cross. He *knows* our condition; he joins our suffering. And these profound descriptions of suffering, whether in the first half of the psalm or in the crucifixion accounts of the four Gospels, conclude with cries of nearly unutterable joy. Because God so fully knows our pain, being with us in our pain whether we feel God's presence or not, God is a power for resurrection, no matter what. In Psalm 22, deepest pain is followed by the exultant cry, "All the ends of the earth shall remember and turn to the Lord," and in the gospels, the pain of Good Friday is prelude to Easter's "he is risen!"

The joyous end to the psalm speaks of praising God in the great congregation, of vows paid. "The poor shall eat and be satisfied; those who seek him shall praise the Lord. May your hearts live forever!" And this great psalm concludes with this acclamation:: "I shall live for [God]!" The one brought low in pain has been raised to exultation, and now proclaims undying love for the Lord who has saved him.

POINTS TO PONDER

Ah, there are "crucifixions" enough in our 21st century world, with repercussions intensifying in every quarter of our existence together. Some are imposed upon us against our will; others to our sorrow claim us as participants. Ponder the issues facing us: name the oppositions and hatreds and blamings and despisings that so torment us in these our troubled times! Then go again to Psalm 22 in light of the gospel accounts of Jesus on that cross. Doesn't Jesus experience the end result of all these issues, which is a death of spirit as well as body? On that cross, Jesus identifies with us, in deepest pain. How do we embrace the fact that God, too, as shown in Jesus, not only knows us, but does so thoroughly, experiencing as well our pains of body and spirit—including the pain of feeling God-forsaken? "Surely not," we cry. And we resist the full impact of incarnation. But can it be that by knowing our pain so deeply God knows as well what resurrections we can bear? Both now and everlastingly? The psalm suggests it, moving suddenly from deepest pain and despair to resurrection joy, with no transition to prepare us for it. Resurrection! Praise and witness tumble from the psalmist, with a witness that shares resurrection joy with sisters and brothers, the congregation, all Israel, and even all the ends of the Earth! God is faithful in steadfast love, bringing us into resurrection joy, no matter the forms of crucifixion we may suffer! Psalm 22 begins in kinship to crucifixion, and ends in the resounding joy and praise of resurrection, and we, even these millennia later, know that because of Good Friday, we live in the promise and reality of Easter, the power and the reality of resurrection! He is risen indeed. Thank God!

CONTEMPORARY PSALM/PRAYER

God in your mercy, hear our prayer.
Your goodness never fails, yet those around us mock your
    holy ways.
Give us grace to remember your steadfast love of the world,
your compassion with those who suffer.
You receive the scorn hurled at those who walk your righ-
teous paths.
You do not turn your face from those who are sick in body
    or spirit.
You sustain the oppressed and those who endure violence.
You walk with those unjustly condemned to die.
You have promised in the abandoned One on the cross
that the abandoned people of the world will have life.
Free us from the fears that assail us, that we may praise you,
joining all who call your name in thanksgiving for your suf-
    fering love.
For your love will prevail. You will rule over all the Earth
and you will "wipe every tear . . . Death will be no more;
mourning and crying and pain will be no more."*
We stand in awe of you, God of life, for you have heard our cry.
Let generation after generation praise your holy name. Amen.

*Revelation 21:4.

— 8th MEDITATION —

PSALM 119

Teach Me, O Lord, the Way
of Your Statutes

Read Psalm 119

I NEVER PAID much attention to this psalm until I undertook my spiritual discipline of reading a psalm each night. But psalm 119! It went on, and on, and on—for 176 verses! So, of course, I spread it across several nights—and it seemed a bit repetitive to me. As I told you, after I finished my first reading of the psalms, I went back to Psalm 1 and continued with my nightly discipline. However, the second time through somehow intensified the psalms—in a sense, they had become my "friends." And eventually I came once again to psalm 119.

In the process of reading each of the 176 verses again, I began to ask, "why so long? Why 176?" This sent me to the Brueggemann/

Bellinger commentary, where my question became my exclamation—of course 176! It's an acrostic of the 22 letters in the Hebrew alphabet! Each of the 22 sections has 8 lines, every one of which begins with the same Hebrew letter. Thus the first group of eight starts each line with aleph, the second group with bet, and so on until the final group, which is the last letter, tau. Because we read it in English, we miss its full meaning. Just as the alphabet includes all letters, even so the law includes all aspects of our lives together within God's covenant.

And that leads to the next obvious question: what exactly *is* this law that is so loved in this psalm? And, of course, it had to have been the law of Moses. For that, one must read again the books of Exodus, Leviticus, Numbers, and Deuteronomy, which detail the laws given to enable Israel to be a community in covenant with God.

Think about it: The Israelites had been slaves for 400 years in Egypt. The only way they knew how to live was through obedience to Pharaoh's slavemasters. They knew how to make bricks, how to do manual labor, how to be subservient. But what did they know about how to be a people on their own, self-governed? How could they BE an independent people unless they learned what it was to govern themselves in ways that created the kind of community where people mattered, where folks knew right from wrong apart from any slavemaster saying "obey" is right and "disobey" is wrong? How could they be self-governing—how could they be anything at all that mattered? No wonder it took forty years in the wilderness! They had to learn how to be a people living together, bound together in covenant with God.

In Exodus 20 we get the first inklings of how they can do this—it is the "ten commandments," also called the "ten Words," introduced with the most elemental foundation: the basic covenant with God, inaugurated by God, who chooses this people as recipients and participants in the covenant. Here is the basic structure for Israel: honoring the God who had brought them out of Egypt, and not pretending some finite idol made with their own hands was worthy of worship. Honoring the very name of God, which is not misusing the divine name in careless conversation or meaningless oaths. Worshiping God in the very structure of life itself: six days you shall labor; but not the seventh. On the seventh, rest! And honor the Lord. Following these three are the seven communal commands: honoring your parents, honoring one another by refraining from murder, from theft, from adultery, from lying, from greed. Don't charge interest when you loan money to a poor person. If you loan something to a neighbor and take your neighbor's cloak as a pledge to repay, make sure you return the cloak at nightfall, lest your neighbor be cold during the night. You shall be a holy people.

This summary of Exodus 20–21 is expanded through Leviticus, Numbers, and Deuteronomy. The book of Numbers also details much of the wandering of the people for forty years—was not this a time to begin practicing what it is to live according to the commandments? The law given in the Torah, the five books of Moses, was in fact the gift of enormous freedom to the new people of Israel, for it was the word of God allowing Israel to BE a people in covenant with God and with one another. The law was the ultimate freedom of knowing how to live together in mutual regard: honor, trust, and trustworthiness. The law, in short, was the ultimate gift of God to the people of God, allowing a ragtag tumble of slaves to become a people, with heads held high, honoring God and their responsibilities to one another in a law-abiding covenantal community. We can see some of the effects of this law in the small book of Ruth, telling the tale of two widows who leave Moab to go to Israel. Two women, with no man to provide for and protect them—how can they survive in a patriarchal world? But the law, Torah, required that the community provide for widows and orphans. Those who owned fields must not gather in the whole of their harvest; they must leave gleanings for the poor, so that the poor might have bread. And we read of Ruth and Naomi gleaning the fields in a compassionate society. The law was gift; the law was freedom; the law was how nobodies can become somebodies. No wonder the psalmist spends 176 verses praising the law as the gift of God for the people of God!

So the law given in the Torah teaches the Israelites how to be a covenant people. However, Psalm 119 is written after the Israelites return from captivity in Babylon. It had been over seventy years since Israel had been a nation. So we look to the book of Nehemiah to see how the returning exiles once again make the transition from being a people without a country, to being Israel again. Nehemiah recounts the return of the exiles, the rebuilding that occurred, and the taking of a census (the results are detailed in Nehemiah 7). And then: "And all the people gathered as one man at the square which was in front of the Water Gate, and they asked Ezra the scribe to bring the book of the law of Moses which the Lord had given to Israel" (Nehemiah 8:1). And Ezra does indeed read, and all the men and women and even the children who had reached the age of understanding listened in awe and joy, weeping their gratitude that now, following the long years of exile under Babylonian rule, they could and would be a covenant community again!

And this is the background to this most amazing Psalm 119. So now when you read Psalm 119, read it with awe for its structure, awe at its lessons, awe at its summation of all the psalms, awe at its wonder. This is the law that we Christians hear summarized in Jesus' "sermon on the mount;" this is the law completely embedded in the double commandment:

> you shall love the Lord your God with all your heart, and
> with all your soul, and with all your mind. This is the

great and foremost commandment. The second is like it. You shall love your neighbor as yourself. On these two commandments depend the whole Law and the Prophets. (Matthew 22:37–40).

Glory be to God for such life-giving laws and commandments!

POINTS TO PONDER

Often, we Christians pit "law" against "gospel," as if never the twain should meet. We treat faith as if it is opposed to the law, as if the law were burdensome rather than being an ultimate expression of the social beauty of loving God and neighbor. Or we think of Paul as if he is absolutely opposing law and gospel, when what he's actually doing is opposing "circumcision" to "baptism." That is, Jesus was Jewish; Christianity begins within Judaism. But the initiating act of Judaism for males is circumcision, so the question arose in early Christianity: must one become Jewish first in order to be Christian? Must gentile men be circumcised in order to become Christian? And Paul rightly sees that for gentiles, baptism is the initiating rite, not circumcision. But Paul never repudiates the law for the Jewish people as expressed in Psalm 119, nor, of course, in Exodus 20, nor the Torah as a whole. To the contrary, he emphasizes the love of God and neighbor that is to mark the new Christian congregations among the gentiles—and as Jesus says, all of the law is summarized (not negated!!) in love of God and neighbor.

If we Christians could move away from the false dichotomy of "law" over against "gospel," we would honor Jewish communities for keeping alive the wonder of the law, too often lost to Christians through the false opposition of law/gospel that became especially prominent in the Reformation.

CONTEMPORARY PSALM/PRAYER

"Blessed are you, Adonai, Creator of the Universe.
You have hallowed us with mitzvot
And commanded us to kindle the light of shabbat."*
Long ago your gift of Torah gave light to your wandering
    children.
Once, like them, we were no people.
Sanctify us, Holy God, and show us the way to be your people,
Joined in hope and assured by your promises.
Enfold us in the peace of sabbath light, in the joy of your
    creation.
Teach us the way that leads to truth. Awaken our senses,
That we may see the beauty of your word and taste its
    sweetness.
Renew in us our desire to seek you with our whole heart,
That we may love you with all our heart, mind, soul, and
    strength.
Grant us grace to love our neighbor even as we love ourselves,
That we may live in faithful communion according to your
    word.
You have given us your word as a lamp to our feet, your
    decrees as a joy in the night.
May we live in the light of God's face and may our song of
    praise never cease.
Amen.

From a traditional Jewish Sabbath prayer.

⁓ 9th MEDITATION ⁓

PSALM 85

Righteousness and Peace Have Kissed Each Other

Read Psalm 85

THE ISRAELITES have returned from their long exile in Babylon—not all at once, but first some, then others, until finally they all are sent back to the land of their fathers and mothers—their own land once more. The books of Ezra and Nehemiah detail some of the restoration that gradually occurs as the people re-establish themselves on their native homeland.

It wasn't easy—those who had been allowed to remain on the land had intermarried with non-Israelites, and with neither temple nor palace nor city walls, what was Jerusalem but a sad memory of the glory it had been? The returning exiles were a lone remnant, but with a hope that they would be the covenant people of God again.

45

Israel had been called into being by God; had received the laws of its covenant from God; Israel was God's people! But seventy years is a long time, and there is no longer an ark of the covenant nor a tent of meeting, let alone a temple. Can they do it? Is God still with them?

Psalm 86 tells the answer. The psalmist laments that the captivity came about because of God's displeasure at Israel's "iniquity," and the 70 long years were punishment for that iniquity. But they have now returned: God brought them back! Is it to be a new beginning, then? Is God's anger abated?

"I will hear what God the Lord will say," says the psalmist, "for God will speak peace to this people . . . that glory may dwell in our land!" But now, for God's answer: don't just read it or listen to it, try to "see" with your mind's eye the amazing vision given to the psalmist in answer to his prayer. For in the silence of bated breath, an amazing thing occurs.

See! There is a stately dance like no other before or after. As if from the shadows, two figures emerge, one from the east and the other from the west. And they bear such names! The first is Steadfast Love and the second is called Truth. They enter from the mists on opposite sides, slowly moving toward one another until they meet. No sooner do they meet when two others emerge: one from the north and the other from the south. They are called Righteousness, and Peace. They also move slowly toward one another until they, too, meet—and kiss each other! East, west, north, south; Steadfast Love, Truth, Righteousness, Peace, all moving toward each other, culminating in a kiss. In this meeting, in this kiss, we have brought the ends of the Earth together, and now it is time for the Heaven above and the Earth beneath to join the dance. Watch now! See Truth, bending down, touching the Earth, and spreading throughout the Earth. And now Righteousness turns, looks up, and begins to rise until finally

Righteousness touches the heavens, spreading throughout the sky. And as you hold your breath and watch, the dance concludes with Steadfast Love, Truth, Righteousness, and Peace pervading the whole land, joined together, entwined in the goodness of God's peace, God's blessing, God's "YES" to the cry of the people once more to be God's own covenant people.

The foundations of their city are Righteousness, Truth, Steadfast Love, and Peace. Bricks and mortar may indeed follow, but in the building of the renewed city there is no mistaking the true foundations. To be God's people, to establish a nation, the foundations are righteousness, truth, steadfast love, and peace.

"Steadfast Love" has a particular meaning in these psalms, for its reference is to God's part in the covenant that God established with Israel. "Steadfast Love" means that God is absolutely unfailing in covenantal love, no matter what. Truth is the solid ground beneath one's feet; righteousness is the overarching reality and the air one breathes. With such ground and such air, love and peace abound. These are the marks of God's blessing, the marks of being truly in covenant with God.

The final coda to the amazing dance? "Indeed, the Lord will give what is good, and our land will yield its produce. Righteousness will go before God, and will make the Lord's footsteps into a Way."

POINTS TO PONDER

The amazing imagery of this psalm applies to all who name themselves a "people of God." In our congregations, in our sanctuaries, don't we gladly own that title? Think about your own congregation. Count the ways that in its own way—in God's way!—it manifests righteousness, truth, love, and peace. And ask yourselves, what are the marks of righteousness? How do you identify that which is righteous? Think about the ways that the Psalms describe righteousness in the way we treat those whom society leaves out. Is this also a description of your congregation?

What about your town, your city? Our nation proudly puts "under God" within our pledge of allegiance. Count the ways you see our United States of America manifesting righteousness, truth, lovingkindness, and peace. Is the "righteousness" of our nation similar to the righteousness described in Psalms? Can you think of improvements, whether in the communities we inhabit or in the larger nation, that might deepen us, "qualifying" us as a "people of God," or "under God"?

It might be worth remembering that the "righteousness" of the Psalms is not the purview of only one religion—for oddly enough (or we might say, by the "grace of God"), religions can feel at home with one another insofar as they value a righteousness that sees to the wellbeing of the "least," an attitude of love that extends to all, a truth that is an honesty with oneself and with others, and a peace that reaches a hand of wellbeing across political, religious, and racial boundaries.

CONTEMPORARY PSALM/PRAYER

Speak peace to us, O God, whose glory fills the Earth.
We cannot recall a time without war abroad and conflict at
    home;
we are exhausted and long for your favor.
Restore us; give us peace beyond our understanding:
Peace that turns swords to plowshares;
peace that turns a shattered land into a home for lovingkindness.
Give us courage to cross the borders we ourselves have made;
bring us together as members of your household,
for you have chosen to live among us, and you give us what
    is good.

Enfold us in the embrace of love and faithfulness;
mark us with the kiss of truth and peace.
Teach us to walk in your paths of righteousness, rejoicing,
for you have turned your anger away from us, and you lean
toward us in joy.
May the glory of your presence remain with us forever. Amen.

— 10th MEDITATION —

PSALM 91

No Evil Shall Befall Thee

Read Psalm 91

S CHOLARS TELL us that psalms 90, 91, and 92 form a triptych, possibly written very soon after the Israelites returned from exile in Babylon. Psalm 90 is ascribed to Moses in order to focus, not simply on the time when Israel was an established people, but on its very beginnings when God used Moses to bring the Hebrews out of bondage in Egypt. God, the eternal and everlasting God, encompasses and surpasses all our histories, all our times—and yet can embrace us even now in our need, although we are but as a passing breeze, a sprig of grass that comes to life in the morning and perishes by evening. Psalm 90 ends with the plea that God will confirm us as we do the work required of us.

And then comes Psalm 91. Indeed, it is God's answering confirmation—first for the Israelites, but extending now even to embrace us, the followers of Jesus the Christ, and to all who "dwell in the shelter of the Most High." It gives a promise that is deeper than pain. The psalm details some of those pains, but more important than the description of peril and pain is the description of the God who shelters us: not now as a King above all kings, nor a Warrior mighty in battle. Those images are supplemented by strength of a different kind: God is imaged as a mother bird, gathering her chicks under her wings, protecting them from harm. The pronouns are masculine—but the image! God gathers us closely, like a mother, gathering her children protectively around her, keeping them safe in her embrace.

And what are the dangers that threaten us? Is it a terror that breaks in at night? Or danger during the day—possibly an arrow—or, bringing the psalm yet closer to home, would it be a gunshot? Is it a pestilence that "stalks in darkness," infecting us without our even knowing—a virus, perhaps, so deadly it could kill us all? Or is it a destruction that lays waste so that a thousand fall at one side, and ten thousand at the other—a war with a destructiveness so massive that it has hardly ever been known before—or perhaps known, but from afar, there being so few survivors. Terror by night, arrows (or gunshots) flying by day, destruction laying waste—ah, there are dangers enough and more, so that we hardly know where we might flee to escape them.

But we read the promise: no evil will befall us . . . God gives angels charge over us, to keep us . . . we will be delivered! Then comes the strange and deep assurance from this God who shelters us beneath her wings: we will call upon God, and God will answer us . . . and *be with us* in trouble. We will have long life and behold God's salvation.

Is it true? All of it? Loved ones die, and we sob our hearts out and grief does not abate; we are stricken with dreadful diseases that take away this or that "essential" ability, and we struggle to overcome; we are plunged into poverty, with no seeming way out. A family is lost, a home is lost, a country is lost—yet we trust in God. Is it true, then? No evil will befall us? How so?

I myself have lived a long life—and like everyone who has managed eight or more decades, I have lived through many a pain and trial. And yes, I have found this psalm's assertions deeply true. It is not possible, given our finitude, to live without pain and loss, but there is a love that is deeper than pain; a presence that endures even in absence; a strength surpassing our finitude and weakness; a health that is deeper than death. The undergirding, everlasting, sustaining God is with us, making it possible for us to go on, keeping us—like a mother bird, shielding her children beneath her wings, no matter what. The experience brings us back to the ancient assurance from Deuteronomy: "underneath are the everlasting arms."

So read Psalm 91 again. Test it against the tragedies, the pestilence, the arrows, the destruction. And then go read Psalm 92, the third of this triptych, and join the affirmation of the psalmist: It is good to give thanks to the Lord, and to sing praises to Thy name, O most High, to declare thy steadfast love in the morning, and thy faithfulness by night.

POINTS TO PONDER

It seems that the ills faced by the psalmist are surpassed and then some by the ills of our own time: sickness and death from a virus that spins its way around the world, ever evolving into more deadly forms? Weapons of destruction thrust like arrows into the atmosphere—but now with the potential to turn millions into ashes and dust in a moment? Enmities, not just between nations, but

within nations, threatening destruction from within? Intensifying
storms that have grown incrementally into massive threats? A planet
heating and drying so rapidly that agriculture is now threatened?
Each of these problems has potential answers, if we have but the
will and the faith to address them collectively as well as individually.
We have brought these ills on ourselves. Can we, like the psalmist,
call upon God to give us the strength and the wisdom and the
courage to address these problems? And can we draw strength
from Psalm 91's promise of divine presence to do what we must?

CONTEMPORARY PSALM/PRAYER

> God our protector,
> we sing of your might and look to you as our fortress.
> We lift our hearts in praise for the home you make for us.
> When the storms of life are raging, you are our shelter.
> Like the mother hen who hides her chicks from the predator,
> you stand against all earthly powers that threaten to undo us.
> Ground us in hope, knowing that in times of trial, God's
>   truth still abides.
> Give us courage to put our trust in you,
> and wisdom to turn our swords to plowshares.
> Grant us grace to be your ministers of reconciliation.
> Raise up among us peacemakers, for you are our dwelling
>   place,
> and in your holy habitation, watched over by angels,
> we live together in peace, nurtured by your love.
> Thanks be to God. Amen.

— 11th MEDITATION —

PSALM 51

Against Thee Only

Read Psalm 51

S URELY IT IS the most fervently cherished of all the psalms, this psalm of contrition! All of us, at one time or another, have prayed our own version of this psalm, using its words and feeling our own particular anguish at the sense in which we, too, come before God dealing with our own "most grievous fault." There is reason indeed that this psalm is included in most Ash Wednesday services, for its contrition covers a multitude of human stumblings, intentional and unintentional. We pray the psalm together and individually at the same time, bent with awareness and grief because of those things corporately and individually that we have done or participated in that work against the good, the holy, the loving—against God. We use these words when our

55

own fail us, for here the psalmist takes us into the deepest places
of the human spirit, and whether we are alone or in the midst of
a praying congregation, we bow in utter contrition.

Verse four takes us to the heart of the confession; hear it:
"Against Thee, Thee only, I have sinned, and done what is evil in
Thy sight . . ." But even in this nadir of despair, another reality whis-
pers its truth. Is it not the case that hidden within every misdeed,
intentional and unintentional, there is a multi-directionality? If
indeed God is omnipresent, feeling the entire being of all beings,
then vicious words, deeds, acts, thoughts toward any creature are
also against God, for God must feel those feelings as well. The
very "awfulness" of sin is this multi-directionality, this ripple effect,
so that what at first seems isolated in its harm actually has effects
beyond itself that multiply the hurt, the pain, the evil. No evil deed
ends in its doing; all evil doing is against God as well as against
creatures. Evil is multi-directional in its effects.

If, as the prologue to Psalm 51 says, the psalm is one of David's
"when Nathan the prophet came to him, after he had gone in to
Bathsheba," then is it not the case that David's "thee only" might
be expanded? We are not given Bathsheba's response to the king's
importunate demand, but she was a young wife. Was she terrified?
Did she have any power to resist the king? Was she, like her husband Uriah, a Hittite and an immigrant to Israel? Dare she even
resist one who had so much power over her? Surely the king sinned
against Bathsheba, as well as against God!

And what of the husband? Was he young, serving in the
military as a way of integrating into Israelite society? Was he
puzzled when suddenly he was sent into the very front line?
Then found himself alone as the others drew back? Was he terrified, knowing the immanence of death? Would he ever see his
young wife again? Surely the king sinned against Uriah when
he planned his murder!

"Against Thee, Thee only have I sinned," cries out the psalmist, with his soul torn in two from the grief and irreversibility of what he has done. Is it too much to ask that he express some grief as well for what he has done to the young Bathsheba? To her husband Uriah? A purpose is served by not naming the victims in Psalm 51, for, as it stands, the very absence (other than "bloodguiltiness") of specificity leaves a certain universality to the psalm—we are left to fill in our own blanks. Perhaps there were other prayers of David not shared with us, in which he agonizes over the specifics of what he did to Bathsheba and Uriah, seeking the release of God's compassion, mercy, and guidance toward next steps.

But we who use this psalm of great confession and contrition might do well, as we pray through its words, to fill in our own specificities of what we have done and to whom, begging God for forms of redress that might yet be taken, whether as an individual or a society.

POINTS TO PONDER

We sin against God and each other simultaneously, whether the "other" be a person, a people, a group deemed "misfit" by a punishing majority; whether the "other" be merely unfortunate, or deeply participant in their own misfortune. Whoever they may be, they matter: to themselves, to God. Our sins work to the ill-being of so many—people, creatures of the earth, and the planet itself. And insofar as God cares for all things—including this planet, its life-forms, its people, us—our sins against any and all is at the same time a sin against God.

The overriding sins facing our nation, whether in the past or present, might be our national (and alas, personal) policies of marginalizing people in order to exploit them, or to steal from them. We convince ourselves that stealing people from Africa in order to force them to work without wages was perfectly permissible since it "helped" our economy—and besides, from time immemorial, even in ancient Israel, those who had the power to do so enslaved others for profit, didn't they? Why not us as well? The egregious wrongs we committed during the centuries of slavery yielded, upon "emancipation," to more invidious forms of exploitation, disempowerment, and enforced poverty through many practices such as restricting educational opportunities and "redlining" properties to make them forbidden to persons of color.

With regard to native peoples who had inhabited this land for centuries prior to our arrival, we pretended not to notice when treaties drawn up with them were disregarded so that we could steal their land, and ensure their poverty as their traditional ways of life were upended.

We assumed that persons of Chinese heritage were privileged to build our railroads with scant pay or accommodations. And in wartime we assumed Americans of Japanese ancestry (not those of German ancestry) should lose most, if not all, of their possessions and be incarcerated in camps, lest they become "traitors."

In addition to these many moral calamities, we systematically ridiculed and despised every new wave of immigrants—even though we all have immigrant ancestry. All of these things, in various scales of horror, were made to seem natural—and the privileged castes who enabled these things were supported through acceptance by the rest of us, to the extent that we viewed such states of affairs as "normal." But as we know today, whether such things describe past or current policies of our nation, social evils multiply and taint for generations.

We have sins and enough to confess. May we have the strength that comes from confession to throw our will and our action toward corrections that can to some extent soften the scars of sin. "Against Thee, and Thee only!" we cry, even as we feel the venom that poisons us all as the cumulative results of sin affect us still. The omnipresent God feels the effects of all our sins. Could we even say "Against Thee, against Thee also have we sinned!" in our prayers of confession? Our God of mercy continues to offer ways of transformation, of new life. Pray God we know enough to recognize these ways, to accept them, and to enact them.

CONTEMPORARY PSALM/PRAYER

> Merciful God, we come to you with contrite hearts;
> We have followed our own devices and desires
> And failed to honor you with our whole mind, strength, and heart.
> We confess that we too often find it convenient
> To overlook the injustice around us rather than speak your truth
> Lord, in your mercy, hear our prayer
> God of love, your whole creation groans in pain, waiting for redemption.
> Teach us to treasure the lives of all your creatures.
> Heal the wounds that we inflict on each other.
> Give us resolve to break the barriers of race and clan.
> Grant us grace to lay down all envy and resentment.
> And to work for your reign of peace.
> Hear the cries of the people; give them relief from conflict,
> And cure all nations' warring madness.
> Grant to our country and its leaders the will to seek your justice
> And to remember the needs of your children.
> Keep us faithful to your Word.
> Wash us in the river of the water of life, that we may walk in newness all our days.

Open our lips, and we will join with all your holy ones,
Praising you, in the song of everlasting peace. Amen.

━ 12th MEDITATION ━

PSALM 72

He Shall Deliver the Poor ... the Needy ... and the Helpless

Read Psalm 72

THIS PSALM is a prayer most likely for King Solomon, given the riches of Israel described in. The book of I Kings amply describes how the reign of Solomon brought Israel to a time of great wealth and sovereignty; nations that previously had been enemies of Israel are now more like satellites, providing slaves for Solomon's many building projects. The prayer that is Psalm 72 describes that prosperity, but intermingled with the descriptions of prosperity are descriptions of the qualities considered essential for Israel's kings.

Look at the rhythm of the psalm: it begins with a prayer that the king shall manifest the righteousness that comes from God and rule through that righteousness. Its first manifestation is that the king shall defend the poor and the needy. As he does this, says the psalm, "the mountains yield prosperity for the people, and the hills [shall bring] righteousness to the people." This sequence, suggesting a causative relationship between how we treat each other and the condition of our natural environment, is typical of ancient Israel's worldview. We are connected, not only to each other, but also to our environment; justice in one area affects justice in the other. The converse is equally so: injustice in the human community adversely affects nature as well.

Next, the psalm expands upon righteousness: the righteous king will defend the children of the poor and punish the wrongdoers. How shall he do this? Remember, in all the descriptions of the law given in the Torah, there is no mention at all of the need to construct prisons for the purpose of punishing and restraining those who break the many laws. To the contrary, every crime receives a punishment appropriate to the crime. Read Exodus 21 and 22 for an example of how this worked. For instance, if two men are engaged in a fist fight of sorts, and one of the men accidentally causes a nearby pregnant woman to fall and have a miscarriage, that man must pay a fine for the loss, with the husband of the woman naming the amount of money due for this misdemeanor (Ex 21:22). In more serious crimes, such as murder or thievery or physical harm, there is a compensating action (Ex 21:23). Every untoward act disrupting the harmony of the community has an appropriate act of recompense, and it is the responsibility of the king to see that justice obtains for the poor as well as for the rich. In this way, the righteousness of the nation is assured.

Following this beginning, the psalm praises the dominion of Israel with the succession of Solomon—nations and their rulers are named as coming to Israel to honor the king. "May all kings fall down before him, all nations do him service" declares the psalmist, which is immediately followed by for he delivers the needy when they call, the poor and those who have no helper. He has pity on the weak and the needy, and saves the lives of the needy. From oppression and violence he redeems their life; and precious is their blood in his sight.

Isn't it interesting that only two issues are named that bring honor and blessing for the king? The first one we would expect: it is the due honor given to the king by others who likewise rule in their own countries: the king's reign is recognized and honored by other kingdoms. We should expect this, shouldn't we? Isn't this the traditional diplomatic relationship among various leaders of nations, be they kings of old or presidents, prime ministers, chancellors, or such today? They hold visits "of state," recognizing one another, building agreements with one another, honoring one another.

But the second issue that brings honor and blessing to Israel's king is surely remarkable. It has nothing to do with honor and glory and riches—to the contrary, it has to do with the poor, the needy, the afflicted. And some of those afflictions are, in fact, inflicted by those who have power and wealth. But the most powerful person of all in the land is now held responsible for redressing such conditions. Rulership is not for the display of power, but for the use of power to lift up the downtrodden, the needy. And to the extent that the ruler does this, that ruler is righteous, and that ruler is blessed.

These descriptions of the righteous king are followed by descriptions of agricultural flourishing; for again, Israel's understanding of righteousness was that the flourishing of nature itself depended upon the righteousness of the whole human community, rich and poor alike.

The psalm ends with blessing: "Blessed be the Lord, the God

of Israel, who alone does wondrous things. Blessed be his glorious name for ever; may his glory fill the whole earth. Amen, and Amen."

Thus ends this psalm, which measures the righteousness of the king by the king's care of the poor and the needy. Insofar as the king is thus righteous, the nation will flourish and all nature will flourish, all thriving under the blessing of the Lord our God.

POINTS TO PONDER

Does it seem strange to us that the value of the king is measured by the king's care of the poor and the needy? Would we ever think of using such standards today to evaluate the competence of our political leaders? Isn't "The Economy" a much better way of discerning good or poor leadership? Surely profits and conveniences outweigh the needs of the poor! Don't they? And besides, isn't it vastly easier to blame the poor and the needy for their poverty and needs? Surely neither we nor our leaders bear any responsibility! But the psalm suggests we do.

And what about the psalm's correlation of justice for the poor and needy with environmental flourishing? Do we relate the deterioration of the natural world to our need for profits and comforts? What are the reasons for polluted, lead-ridden drinking water in the faucets of poor communities? What are the rationales for "toxic dumps" and their placement? Why are mountains razed and the inhabitants of once beautiful lands stuck with toxic leftovers? Or perhaps we blame energy companies for wanton practices that lay waste to the land, in the name of higher and higher profits. But isn't it the populace as a whole, we who are dependent on the wonders of cheap energy to cool and heat our homes, to make convenient throwaways, who depend upon gasoline for our cars, trucks, and machines—aren't we part of the problem as well?

Yet another issue raised by the psalm is the responsibility of the ruler for righteousness and justice in the land, measured precisely by how well the ruler redresses the afflictions of the poor and needy. Can you imagine political campaigns in our own country if candidates for the presidency or congress proudly proclaimed how they have addressed, and would continue to address, the plight of the poor in the country? . . . and the children of the poor? . . . or the sick? Ah, that politicians would add such actions to their reasons for election or reelection! What kind of a country that would be!

CONTEMPORARY PSALM/PRAYER

Blessed be the Lord, the God of Israel who alone does wondrous things.
Your prophets, O God, delivered your word in the time of kings,
And instructed them in your ways of justice and righteousness.
Grant us courage that we may choose just leaders
And hold them accountable according to your word.
Give us leaders who listen to our hopes for all people to prosper;
Let them know we pray to you, seeking deliverance and redemption for all.
Help us as a nation to feed the poor and defend their cause,
And to see our wellbeing as joined to the wellbeing of the vulnerable among us
Bless us all our days with justice and mercy, falling like rain on our land,
Where the lives of school children are precious in our sight,
Where those wrongly accused are precious in our sight,
Where the forgotten ones are precious in our sight,
Where righteousness flourishes and peace abounds.

Blessed be your name forever; may your glory fill the whole Earth. Amen.

⌐ 13th MEDITATION ⌐

PSALM 44

Why Dost Thou Sleep, O Lord?

Read Psalm 44

H AVE YOU ever felt as if your prayers are not only unan-
swered, but as if they are like one of those awful hot-air
balloons that simply hit the ceiling and bounce back,
eventually just falling limply to the floor with no life left in them?
We doggedly plow on, dragging our faith behind us, but our spirits
are low; it's as if we are just in this thing alone, with despair on
every side. Are we even faithful persons if there is neither comfort
in prayer, nor hope for efficacy in prayers that seem to go nowhere?
Psalm 44 takes us into such a painful realm of the spirit. "Why
dost thou sleep, Lord?" is a painful cry of both despair and hope,
hardly matched in any other psalm.

The psalm begins positively enough, recounting "the olden days," when God led this people to victory after victory, establishing them in the land. But that was "then"! What of "now"?

Hear the despair of the psalmist in the context of military defeat, social havoc, and dishonor:

> You have rejected us, and abased us, and have not gone out
> with our armies. You have made us turn back from the foe,
> and our enemies have taken spoil for themselves. You have
> made us the taunt of our neighbors, the derision and scorn
> of those around us. You have made us a byword among
> the nations, a laughing-stock among the peoples. All day
> long my disgrace is before me, and shame has covered my
> face at the words of the taunters and revilers, at the sight
> of the enemy and the avenger. (44:9–16)

Anger mingles with despair until the psalmist finally cries out—in an echo of Elijah's words to the priests of Baal—"Rouse yourself! Why do you sleep, O Lord? Awake, do not cast us off forever!"

What do we do with such despair? The psalmist certainly gives us one answer to such a question. Name it, and fight with God. The psalmist goes further—he *blames* God! "Why did *you* let this happen?" Ah, and isn't there a familiar ring to that accusation? Haven't we, too, blamed God? "We prayed, and he died anyhow!" "We trusted you, and look what happened!" "We begged you to stop the fires—now our town is gone!" "It's YOUR fault, God, YOURS!" And we cry with anger and despair intermingled.

Perhaps we resort to "reality" and say against such feelings that we can hardly blame God for our despair. Surely it is simply our circumstances. Our finitude! Our political situation, our private situations of terrible loss, our embarrassments at failures, our feelings that we have not truly lived up to a high calling, that whatever we

do to help others in these hard times is barely a drop in the proverbial bucket and nothing changes. We deal with overwhelming
tragedies, personal and national and international and planetary.
We participate in failures of our own making, as well as social and
political failures. What right have we to bring them to God, much
less even seem to blame God? For that's what the psalmist certainly
seems to be doing. It's as if the psalmist were saying "It's all YOUR
fault, God!" And, then, having said the awful thing, saying what
it's like when it seems as if God has forgotten us: "we sink down
to the dust; our bodies cling to the ground." Despair is like that.
It drags us down into dust, and we feel like dust, worthy only to
be swept away and cast into some worthless dustheap.

And yet. . . and yet! The last verse of the psalm is this: "Rise
up! Come to our help! Redeem us for the sake of your steadfast
love!" Hope? Is this not hope rising from despair? And is it not
faith, daring to name God to be a God who is steadfast, whose
love is deepest kindness? What then, of our despair? The lesson of
the psalmist is that life is an intense mixture of joy and sorrow, of
success and of failure, of despair and hope, and that we are called to
recognize and embrace both ends of the spectrum, taking them into
this thing we call faith. Surrounding our faith and undergirding
it is the deep knowledge of our souls, of our whole being, that we
serve and worship a God who can handle the whole of who we
are, a God who *is* steadfast love—indeed, a God who "slumbers
not nor sleeps."

So what we do with our despair? Let it drag us more deeply
into itself? No. Like everything else—and like the psalmist—we
bring it to God. And here's the curious thing: despair itself can
be embraced in a life of faith as one of the dimensions of our full
humanity. And one of the curiosities of a life of faith is that despair
can even deepen faith as it senses its own boundaries, and yields
once more not simply to hope, but to places of calmness in our

spirits that are deeper yet than either joy or despair: depths that embrace despair and hope together.

POINTS TO PONDER

When pandemics sweep the world, when politics threaten to tear us all apart, when truth crumbles before challenges endlessly threatening the possibility of knowing anything clearly, when military "might" acknowledges error and defeat, we do what we always do; we do what the psalmist does—we bring it to God. And having done so—or even in and through the process of doing so—we do what we know is necessary. We look not to global issues, but to local ones: who in our community suffers? What good can we do to alleviate suffering? Is it just presence? Is it working in food pantries? Is it visiting the sick? Is it helping someone to arrange health care? Is it helping a small child learn to read? Or does responsive care look to ways individuals and groups of individuals can address global problems—recycling? Arguing for fewer plastics? Insisting upon clean drinking water? There is power in kindness; there is power in mercy; there is power in caring. The power is magnified when the kindness and mercy and caring of individuals is multiplied through community. Despair blocks us into isolated inactivity; hope releases us for acts of kindness. Choose hope—and watch for what transformations may happen. And trust in God, who neither slumbers nor sleeps.

CONTEMPORARY PSALM/PRAYER

> Mighty God, hear our cries, for we are a desperate people.
> We see the innocent dead in the streets, victims of brutal war;
> we read the names of those unjustly killed in our own land.
> We ask, "Are you sleeping, God?"

Where can we place the blame?

Who are the ones whose eyes are closed;

whose ears cannot hear your call to live in peace with our
neighbors?

What keeps us from walking the path that leads to your
reign of life?

God, you are the mother of all compassion,

the father of all consolation, our strong deliverer.

Lift the clouds of fear; let the light of your face shine on us
again.

Comfort those who grieve and those who are dying.

Sustain the sick, the poor, and those in trouble of any kind.

Banish from our hearts all greed and envy

that we may revere the lives of all who live on Earth.

Rise up, O God, and embrace us with your steadfast love.
Amen.

～ 14th MEDITATION ～

PSALM 88

Why Dost Thou Hide Thy Face from Me?

Read Psalm 88

WE HAVE in Psalm 88 one of the strangest psalms in the entire psalter. This psalm, like many, is a lament: despair! But the format varies from all the other laments, because this psalm includes no answer from God. Watch the movement of the psalm.

In verses one through five, we see the severe plight of the psalmist—and it is dire indeed. He is ill, desperately ill, and he cries out to God day and night. It's almost as if he has become a dead person, practically in the grave, forsaken!

In verses six through nine, the psalmist now blames God: it is *God* who has done thus and so to him! YOU, God, have put me in the lowest pit! YOUR wrath rests upon me. YOU have afflicted me with all YOUR waves. YOU, God, have removed all my acquaintances from me, and YOU God, are the one who has made me an object of loathing.

Have you ever dared to say such things to God? Blamed God for all your sickness and troubles? Is it deepest trust that allows the psalmist to yell at God, confident nonetheless that he is safe in God's hands—even though he blames God for having done, or permitted to be done, all these things now against him? Is this miserable confession of despair at the same time a mode of trust? Can despair ever be a mode of trust?

But move now to the middle verses of the psalm, which are not much of an improvement on the first. Verses ten and eleven almost taunt God. In essence the psalmist says, "Look, God. What use am I to you in the grave? Can I praise you from the grave? Can I declare your 'steadfast love' from the grave? Will your 'wonders' be made known in the grave? The grave is a land of forgetfulness! Who can possibly praise your righteousness there?" The unspoken rejoinder here might be, "you might as well let me live—I'm of much more use to you alive than dead!" How dare one talk to God like that? Well, the psalmist dared to talk like that . . . and those who originally compiled these psalms thought it a worthy enough psalm to be included. Perhaps God can handle that sort of emotion. Perhaps we don't have to "hold back" in prayer to God. Perhaps "dreadful honesty" is really the best policy!

And we come to the final verses, thirteen though eighteen. Normally this would be where the lament gives way to thanksgiving, for God's answer to prayer. But not in this strange psalm of lament; there is no redress here. Rather, the psalmist gives a reprise of his complaint, as in verses thirteen and fourteen: I've cried out to you for help every morning; why do you reject me and hide your face from me? Note that the complaint is also accusation, as in the psalm's beginning. And verses fifteen through seventeen simply intensify the problem. The psalmist has indeed been afflicted from youth, overcome by terrors sent to him— by God? Yes, if all things come from God! God's burning anger has passed over him; God's terrors have destroyed him, surrounding him like water all day long—he is about to drown in the terrors God has inflicted upon him.

And finally, the last straw in the closing verse: "You have caused friend and neighbor to shun me; my companions are in darkness." Thus ends this psalm of lament: all misery, all blame, all abandonment, and all addressed to a God who has apparently thoroughly rejected him. And yet, and yet! This psalm is in fact a prayer. Even in the depths of feeling God-forsaken, the psalmist prays. He continues to trust.

POINTS TO PONDER

They matter, these psalms we so seldom include in public worship; they matter. Psalm 88 may be the saddest of all the psalms, for it ends where it begins, in a feeling of abandonment by God.

Yet this feeling of abandonment does not lead the psalmist to abandon God. Rather, the psalmist rails at God, accusing God, all the while crying out for God—who does not apparently care. Regardless! The psalmist cares. And he names the God he thinks has forsaken him: God is filled with steadfast love, kindness, and God is faithful; God is righteous. Even in despair, the psalmist rightly names God. In the midst of anger and despair, the psalmist trusts.

What does this have to do with our twenty-first century horrors, our idiocies, our angers, our forsakenness? This unending psalm of lament tells us that even in the deepest trials that could or even should challenge our faith—the answer is trust. Honesty. Pray anyhow. Faith in the steadfast love of God. Faith in the righteousness of God. Faith that dares to believe in the Light even in the midst of what appears to be unending Darkness. Trust anyhow. Believe.

And it may be that while the psalmist receives no answer in this particular lament, that is precisely why it is included in the psalter. Surely, we can turn to those other laments that leave us feeling vindicated in our faith, our trust. But perhaps our souls need this psalm 88 precisely because it so reflects back to us our own situation. Oddly enough, it comforts us because it is as if God through this psalm nonetheless embraces our despairing spirits and gives us hope. Like this despairing psalmist, we trust God. Regardless.

CONTEMPORARY PSALM/PRAYER

Compassionate God
We look for streams of living water in desert lands,
But we find only desolation and confusion.
We cry to you through all the trouble of our days.
We cry for peace and there is none in our hearts.
In the depths of our despair, we fear we are below your reach,
But still we call to you.
When we cannot pray with words, hear our sighs.
When we cannot hear your voice,
Let us know your sorrow, deep as our own.
Our hope lies in calling your name, O God.
You turn your face from us, but your presence never ceases.
You are the One who knows us by our name;
Who can redeem us from floods of terror that threaten to
    overwhelm us.
We pray for peace in your name, peace beyond our under-
    standing. Amen.

— 15th MEDITATION —

PSALM 65

The Dawn and the Sunset Shout for Joy!

Read Psalm 65

PSALM 65 reads as an antidote to the despair of Psalms 44 and 88, for it is basically a psalm of absolute thanksgiving, absolute joy, absolute trust. Within Judaism the psalm functions as a harvest hymn and a prayer for the winter rains to replenish the Earth.

The first stanza focuses on us in our relation to God. The psalm praises God, who answers prayer, to whom all people come. And God forgives our transgressions, blesses us, and brings us to dwell in God's courts. And there we will be satisfied with the goodness of God's house, God's holy temple. Imagine the wonder of it! We belong to God, who embraces us in care, forgiveness, and welcome. In God's house we are no strangers, we are at home. And oh, what an amazing privilege it is to be at home in the house of God, who bids us welcome.

In the second stanza we move away from the cherishing of being at home with God, lifting our eyes higher than even the house of God. For the very God who welcomes us is in fact Lord of all the Earth. We serve a creator God of all nature and of all people, who establishes mountains, stills the roaring of the seas, and the tumult of the peoples. To the ends of the Earth, people stand in awe of the signs of God—and even the gateways to the morning and the evening, the dawn and the sunset, shout for joy! Haven't you almost heard, and surely seen, the dawn and/or sunset shouting for joy? Haven't you seen a sunset so glorious that it stops you in your tracks, thrills you with yet again a display of sheerest beauty? Doesn't delight in the beauty of God's creation rise up in your soul, overwhelming you with wonder? What delight! What absolute delight!

The effect of God's lordship is that God visits the Earth and causes food to grow, water to flow to nourish people, beasts, and all growing things. Hills gird themselves with rejoicing, meadows are clothed with flocks, and valleys are covered with grain.

Because of all this, in all of this, the whole of creation—including us—shouts for joy; yes, we sing! Whereas Psalms 44 and 88 nearly plunged us into despair, Psalm 65 lifts us to mountaintops as we sing this psalm of sheer joy and thanksgiving.

POINTS TO PONDER

So we have looked at three psalms consecutively, two of increasing despair, and the third of deepest joy and thanksgiving. We could learn from the psalms of despair the lesson to trust no matter what, of faith that is deeper than doubt, of courage to speak one's despair, to voice it to God, regardless.

Are there likewise lessons to be learned from this psalm of thanksgiving? It is the case, is it not, that all three psalms speak to our deepest spirits? Not one of the three is a stranger to us, neither the constrictions of 44 and 88 nor the expansiveness of 65. And most of the time we live somewhere between the emotions. Each is familiar, each echoes in our souls—but our everydays tend to be more prosaic affairs. And perhaps that's what everydayness is about: knowing both extremes, appreciating both extremes, and drawing from both for the ordinary living of our days, weaving together somehow the heights and the depths in the midst of the ordinary. We do our daily tasks, tend to those in our care, laugh or weep with friends, plan great or little things to be accomplished. And all the while in this ordinariness we are aware of the extremes, which are part of the edges of our lives—but sometimes, as with the psalmist, they move to the very center.

It is enough to know that both are embraced in a life of faith. And sometimes, we see this even in the ordinariness of our church, our community of faith, which seems to be so steady, so "ordinary" in its very steadiness. So we thank God for "ordinariness," knowing that it *is* ordinary only because we also know its edges of despair and delight. Thus we thank God for the extremes of delight and despair, and for the ordinariness that holds them both somehow together.

CONTEMPORARY PSALM/PRAYER

Ever-present God, we are thankful always to be at home
  with you.
You welcome us into your courts where goodness abides,
  where there are no strangers, and where friends rejoice in
  peace.
When we are overwhelmed by failure and feel unworthy of

your glory,
you offer forgiveness and make us glad by your gracious
presence,
for you have made your home with mortals and chosen to
dwell among us.
Open our hearts to your holy presence that permeates the
Earth you love:
We lift our eyes to the hills and remember your strength and
steadfast love,
We search the depths of your mercy like clear, flowing streams.
We look to the fields and pastures that you adorn with glorious bounty,
revealing the extravagance of your gifts that sustain the Earth
and its creatures.
Give us joyful songs to greet the dawn's bright hues that
herald each new day,
and gladness to welcome the sunset's splendor, the gateway
to a peaceful night.
Grant us grace to walk with you in humbleness,
to offer healing to those who suffer,
to make home for the homeless,
as you have made home for us.
In praise and thanksgiving to our God, the hope of all the
Earth. Amen.

— 16th MEDITATION —

PSALM 30

Joy Comes with the Morning

Read Psalm 30

THIS PSALM tells a story. It begins with triumph, then recounts the reason for triumph: God has healed the psalmist from his recent illness and closeness to death. Exultation comes with the return of health, leading to this memorable song of praise to God: God's anger is but for a moment, but God's favor is for a lifetime. Weeping may last the night, but "joy comes with the morning!" Is this not a psalm of delight, of joy at overcoming illness, and of the presence of God in time of need?

The psalmist follows this stanza by suggesting the story behind his recent illness. He had been reveling in his own prosperity, smugly confident that his good fortune was permanent. For hadn't it come as a blessing from God? But as the psalmist turned to his possessions as the foundation of his wellbeing, the "face of God" receded—and the psalmist fell ill. What good were his valued possessions to him then? His possessions were useless for what he really needed, which was the return to health. The grave ("pit") loomed ever closer. All his vaunted possessions were useless. They could not heal him. So he cries out to God—and even chides God. In effect, he says "what good am I to you on Earth once I'm dead? Will the dust praise you?" But then he turns once more to God as the true source of his wellbeing, imploring God's help—and his prayers are answered. Chastened, he returns to health. What he has learned is that his true wellbeing is not in what he possesses, but in whom he trusts.

The final stanza is sheerly praise, sheerly delight: "You have turned my mourning into dancing; you have taken off my sackcloth and clothed me with joy so that my soul may praise you and not be silent. O Lord my God, I will give thanks to you forever!" He has learned the true source of his wellbeing.

POINTS TO PONDER

We live in such a different time! One might be thinking on reading this psalm, "well, today we could simply use our possessions to hire the best physician to book us into the best hospital to receive the best drugs so that we can recover and get on with our lives." We shudder at the crassness of such a thought. But is it not the case that wealth and prestige make extraordinary healthcare resources available? The needs are the same, so why are healthcare benefits constrained by wealth? Isn't there a "commonweal"?

Yet again, what in fact is the basis of our wellbeing? The psalmist makes a transition from dependence upon possessions to dependence upon God. We might prefer a "both/and" proposition!

But the psalm suggests otherwise. It suggests that we examine the basis of our being, the foundation of our lives, the quality of our souls. How do we define, or recognize even, what it is that truly functions as the basis of our wellbeing? Perhaps, suggests the psalm, it might be a good thing to find out. And as we do, perhaps we might begin to ask even more effectively how it is that we might live in a "commonweal" where all have access to the care they need.

CONTEMPORARY PSALM/PRAYER

Gracious God, giver of all good gifts,
you have said our hearts will be wherever our treasure is:
Hear the prayers of our hearts.
Free us from pride in what we acquire or what the world
    approves.
Tune our hearts to your merciful kindness.
Give us grace to treasure the wellbeing of others
and find our wealth in seeing the hungry fed,
the sick healed, the oppressed go free.
By the power of your Spirit, keep us strong and constant
that we may find life and health in the communion of your
    love.
For your mercy that falls on us like gentle rain,
for the joy that comes with the morning,
for the gladness that turns our mourning to dancing,
for your favor that never ends:
we give you thanks and praise, now and forever. Amen.

17th MEDITATION

PSALM 69

Rescue Me from Sinking in the Mire

Read Psalm 69

WHAT A CRY of pain is this psalm, written by one who had seen with horror the destruction of the temple in Jerusalem, who had taken the long march to Babylon, and finally who cried out to God from the very depths of pain. The temple in Jerusalem had been God's own habitation, the witness to God's presence with this people—what despair in its wanton destruction! Without the temple there is no place of Presence, no place for sacrifice, no place for worship. Yes, God is more than the temple, more than walls can contain—but how can one have access to God if the designated place of divine presence is destroyed? And the psalmist, whose heart and soul writhe in the agony of loss, cries out his lament. And the "reward" for this cry of lament?

Taunting.Laughter. Blaming. All in the marketplace of this strange new country.

So this psalmist retreats within himself, questioning himself in the light of these taunts. He knows his own folly, his own failings, and he prays that he himself now expressing his agony shall not in and through this crying cause harm to anyone else. There is harm enough and more to go around! May he not contribute any more to it. But he fears his very openness in his grief and despair might cause pain to others. "My zeal for your house has been my undoing, the reproaches of those who revile you have fallen upon me! When I wept and fasted, I was reviled for it; I made sackcloth my garment; I became a byword among them. Those who sit at the gate [the marketplace] talk about me, and I am the taunt of drunkards." Despair!

And yet: he prays, and in the process he recounts again what he has learned about his God—Israel's God: abundant faithfulness, sure deliverance, great steadfastness, abundant mercy! *This* is the God to whom he prays, the God in whom he trusts above all else, even when all seems to have fallen away. And he begs this God to deliver him, to rescue him "from sinking in the mire." Naming this God, he then names himself, confessing his despair, and not so incidentally castigating those who taunt him, wishing that they also would experience pain and despair.

At last, having exhausted himself in prayer, he moves away from being so totally enmeshed in it—he has, in fact, been "rescued from the mire" in and through his mindfulness of the nature of God. And while the temple is gone, and with it the sacrificial offerings, there is more to the worship of God than sacrificial offerings. There is praise, there is thanksgiving, there is life lived in accordance with kindness and faithfulness and mercy.

And so finally, our psalmist's spirit is indeed raised from despair to hope:

God will deliver Zion, and rebuild the cities of Judah;
they shall live there, and inherit it; the offspring of his
servants shall inherit it, those who cherish God's name
shall dwell there.

Despair gives way to hope, and hope restores one's spirit. These
last triumphant verses declare that our psalmist has been rescued
from the mire!

POINTS TO PONDER

Who has not fallen into despair? The psalmist had lost his country,
and we are threatened with the loss of our own—not from outside
nations determined to conquer us, but from internal threats woven
from lies born of hysteria and grievance, threatening to destroy
this union once and for all from within. We manufacture "realities"
disconnected from facts, and truth disappears in a sticky web of lies,
sucked dry of relevance by the spiders who reap immense wealth
from our gaping gullibilities. And in such a state of disrepair, we
continue our love affair with weapons of death, so that by now
there are far more guns in America than people. Why are we so
ready to kill each other? In self-defense, we may cry—but where
is the "self-defense" when young men barely out of boyhood buy
assault guns, storm into schools, and murder children and teachers
with mad abandon? Why is it so easy to buy these dreadful devices,
and use them? What is happening to us—what are we *allowing*
to happen to us? Who can save us from ourselves? We sink in the
mire of despair.

CONTEMPORARY PSALM/PRAYER

God of our ancestors,
You have witnessed the treaty of mighty rulers,

The schemers who disrupt the righteous and reward the
   wicked.
You have heard the cries of those betrayed by trusted friends,
Help us now in this time of agonizing brokenness,
when family talk is cautious for fear of rancor and discord,
When friends use words as weapons and disregard the wounds.
Calm us when those who know the truth refuse to change.
Guide us through the raging wind and tempest.
Give us wings to fly to you in prayer that we may rest.
Grant us peace in knowing you sustain us, and we will not
   be moved.
We put our trust in you, our God who restores and reconciles
For you will reign now and forever. Amen.

~ 18th MEDITATION ~

PSALM 145

One Generation Shall Praise
Thy Works to Another

Read Psalm 145

PSALM 145 functions as both a closure and a "bridge" within the psalter. The Psalms are divided into five "books," somewhat diffusely related to the time when those particular psalms were organized, and who did the organization. Psalm 145, identified as a psalm of David, is placed as the closing psalm in the final book, which is distinctive in its inclusion of what are called "psalms of ascent," those hymns that pilgrims sang as they walked up the hills of Jerusalem to God's holy temple at the summit. But 145 does not conclude the psalter as a whole. That task is given to the final five psalms, which together amount to a wondrous "Hallelujah Chorus," summing up the basis of all our praise, namely,

89

the nature of God. Psalm 145 looks back to the content of Psalms, and forward to the sheer praise of God.

Psalm 145 begins, appropriately, with a doxology. We will praise God forever; great is the Lord, and greatly to be praised. And then the psalm instructs us well: "One generation shall praise thy works to another, and shall declare thy mighty acts." Think about it. Is not this the work of every parent and grandparent, and of every blessed Sunday school teacher in our congregations, and of all the teachers of "religion" from early childhood to doctoral degrees? Isn't every pastor concerned that every sermon shall impress the congregation with the wonder of God? Doesn't every sermon teach, either implicitly or explicitly about the nature of God? The psalm details for us just who God is for us, and it is almost more than we can take in.

The Lord is gracious and merciful, slow to anger, and great in steadfast love. How often "steadfast love" is mentioned throughout the psalms, and here as we move toward the doxology, God's love is the first thing raised for thanksgiving and praise. God is faithful to the covenant with Israel; God is absolutely dependable. God's love is steadfast, never conditional, stemming not from a response to creaturely conduct, but from the depths of God's own nature. The Lord is good to all, and God's mercies are over ALL God's works. Neither this goodness nor this mercy is arbitrary, not a now-you-see-it-now-you-don't sort of thing. Rather, goodness and mercy stem from the depths of God's nature. And this psalm dares to describe the depths of God's nature—to voice its wonder, to marvel at its expanse, to almost gasp at the deep love of God and its corollary, divine faithfulness to the covenant established with Israel. Surely this is too wonderful for us; it is high, we can barely grasp it. Yet the psalmist asserts it. And we can believe it.

In response, says the psalmist, "all thy works shall give thanks to thee, O Lord." Do you wonder how this can occur? Do the trees give God thanks, do the flowers and grains and vegetables; do the beasts of the field, the birds of the air? Do insects and creeping things? And the psalm suggests that their very being is their thanks to God. Is it so, then, that just by being who God created us to be, we are in our being a thanks to God? The psalmist answers such a question: "Thy godly ones shall bless Thee, they shall speak of the glory of thy kingdom and talk of thy power, to make known to all Thy mighty acts."

And now we come to the conclusion of Psalm 145; it should be familiar to us:

> The Lord sustains all who fall, and raises up all who are bowed down; the eyes of all look to thee, and thou dost give them their food in due time . . . The Lord is righteous in all ways, and kind in all deeds; the Lord is near to all who call upon God . . . God will hear their cry and will save them.

And this psalm finally concludes, "My mouth will speak the praise of the Lord, and all flesh will bless God's holy name forever and ever." Amen! Amen, indeed!

POINTS TO PONDER

In a sense, Psalm 145 begins with a commission and takes the next five psalms—the final psalms—to answer that commission. The commission, of course is to tell the story, to take these ancient texts and translate them into the way we live, the way we think, the way we talk. If creatures without speech nonetheless give thanks to God simply by being, aren't there ways we humans are to show our thanks to God in more than words, but in how we live and act? Do our words show their truth by their conformity to our ordinary ways of being?

The psalms, of course, are communally oriented, not simply individually oriented. And it's easier for us to point to our faith communities as places where each generation praises God's works to the next generation through sermons and lessons. But the final story is always the one that goes deeper than words. It's told in how we extend lovingkindness to those we consider "other": those of different economic status, different religions, different politics, as well as those who hunger, who are lonely, who are needy. It's an enormous commission: how do we and/or our faith communities live it out?

CONTEMPORARY PSALM/PRAYER

Gracious God, we join with all your works in giving thanks.
We are speechless before your unsearchable greatness,
    awed by your power and your compassion.
Our songs of praise, raised hands, and meagre offerings
are not enough to convey the magnitude of your mighty acts,
    your faithful care, and the splendor of your love.
Teach us to pray as we ought;
    give us memory and language to recount your deeds
    that our words may resound to the next generation.
Let our lives echo your goodness.
Send us to uphold the falling and feed the hungry;
    open our ears to hear the cries of those in distress
    and our hands to comfort and care for every living thing.
Grant us grace to speak your praise and bless your holy name
        forever. Amen.

∼ 19th MEDITATION ∼

PSALM 146

The Lord Sets the Prisoners Free

Read Psalm 146

THE DOXOLOGY of these final psalms begins with the importance of trusting God, and the reasons for trusting God. If we put our trust in "creatures," even when we view them as experts of various kinds, we must reckon with the fact that they, like us, are finite, prone to error and self-interest. Indeed, they may even be "humble" servants, striving for the public good—but they, like all of us, will fall prey to error, accident, illness, death. But God! God alone is our hope—God, who made the heavens and Earth. Who keeps faith forever.

And then this psalm of deepest love, deepest praise, moves into the "why" of our trust in God—and this "why" is more than

93

because God is the Creator who has brought into being the heavens
and the Earth. The "why" is because of the very nature of God,
proven time and again.

> God keeps faith forever . . .
> God executes justice for the oppressed . . .
> God gives food for the hungry . . .
> God sets the prisoners free . . .
> God opens the eyes of the blind . . .
> God lifts up those who are bowed down . . .
> God loves the righteous . . .
> God watches over the strangers . . .
> God upholds the orphan and the widow . . .
> But the way of the wicked God brings to ruin.

Do you see what the psalmist does in this extraordinary description of how God acts? The acts of God flow from the nature of
God, and from the depths of the divine nature flows an unending
river of steadfast love, of compassion, of caring even for the least
until we must confess that in God's eyes, there IS no least. None
so low as to be beyond divine care. How is it even possible for us
to regard any creature as "least" if those we are tempted to view
as "least" are, in fact, precious to God?

Furthermore, note that immediately following the holy listing
of those within the divine care is the ruin of "the way of the wicked."
And don't you see that the "wicked" are indeed "wicked" precisely
because they work against the divine care for the oppressed, the
hungry, the prisoners, the bowed down, the stranger, the orphan,
and the widow? Insofar as they participate in opposing the needs
and good of any in this list, they oppose God. Oh, that we should
use the words of this doxology as we evaluate the qualifications of
any person desiring a position of leadership or authority among us.

And so this portion of the doxology speaks of the righteousness

of God, which must be read in relation to the list of the oppressed.
It leads directly into Psalm 147's account of God as the one who
"heals the brokenhearted, and binds up their wounds." Let your
reading of Psalm 146 take you directly into Psalm 147, which elab-
orates on 146 and prepares you for Psalm 148.

POINTS TO PONDER

As noted in this response to Psalm 146, consider its import for the
way we select our leaders. Can you even imagine a prospective
leader who not only speaks to the plight of the oppressed, the
hungry, the prisoners, the blind, the bowed down, the strangers,
the orphan, and the widow, but proposes ways to address these
plights? If we even elected such a candidate for office, would we
judge such a candidate on whether or how such promises were ful-
filled, or would we focus instead on things such as the economy and
international relations? Why should such interests be conflicting?

Moving from the national scene to the local scene of our
faith communities, how do we evaluate those given positions of
authority and leadership? How do we evaluate our pastors? Our
teachers? Our committees and persons in authority? Would a list
such as that given in Psalm 146 even enter our consideration?
Why or why not?

Also, has it occurred to you that the list of items describing God
in this psalm differ from the more traditional Christian descriptions of God's nature in our most popular creeds, the Apostle's
and the Nicene? They begin by describing first the almighty power
of God, and then assert the work of the triune God: the Father in
creating, the Son in terms of death and resurrection, and the Spirit's
work in the community. Discuss the contrasts between Psalm 146
and the creeds as two ways of describing God. How do they come
together? What do you make of their divergences?

CONTEMPORARY PSALM/PRAYER

God of mercy, your love never fails.
Jesus preached what psalms and prophets long ago declared:
Our loving God resolves to bring good news to the poor,
sight to the blind, and release to the prisoner.
Turn us away from those who claim power of their own
    making,
those who create prisons of dependency, forced labor, and
    false hopes.
Give us eyes to see and hearts to share the goodness of your
    abundant love,
the brilliance of your light that drives away the shadows of
    captivity.
You have freed us to live in your mercy: For your name's sake,
grant us grace to care for strangers and lift the downtrodden,
for you have made heaven and Earth, the sea and all that
    lives therein,
and we will praise you our whole life long. Amen.

— 20th MEDITATION —

PSALM 148

God Commanded and They Were Created

Read Psalm 148 and Genesis 1

THE PSALMS deal with nearly all human emotions imaginable, all within the context of the praise of God. And the God being praised is the God of Genesis 1, who is as well the God pointed to in the Pentateuch as a whole. So if you read Psalm 148 carefully, and then Genesis 1, you will see that in Genesis, God calls creation into being through a Word. God speaks, and creation responds by becoming that which God has called it to be. And then if you read Psalm 148 carefully, you will see that it is creation's answering call to God. God calls, creation becomes; creation calls back—that which it has become is now turned into praise of the God who has called it into being. Psalm 148 is creation's answer to Genesis 1. An exquisite bonding ensues, God and creation in covenant together, through call and response. This universal covenant, one could suppose, undergirds and empowers all subsequent communal covenants through which God continuously calls peoples into becoming.

The whole of the Hebrew Bible speaks of God's call to the Hebrew people, uniquely calling them and empowering them to be God's people, in covenant with God whose covenantal promise is steadfast love and faithfulness. The responding affirmation is two-fold. It is Israel's acceptance of the covenantal call in the Passover, and it entails as well Israel's affirmation of the Torah, summarized in the ten life-giving Words of the covenant. Indeed, the shining Face of God shown to Moses on Sinai shines again through Torah—the Face of God for the Jewish people. Through Torah, in its life-giving covenantal laws, the people see the Face of God.

The New Testament speaks of a subsequent people, gentiles, responding to the Jew who is called Jesus, the Christ, through whom we become a new covenantal people with a unique seal, variously called "the Lord's Supper" or "Eucharist." "This is my blood of the covenant," says Jesus, "which is poured out for many." Jesus summarizes Torah in the beatitudes and in his repetition of the summary of the law given in Deuteronomy 6:5 and Leviticus 19:18: love of God and neighbor. Indeed, in the very being of Jesus, we Christians too see the Face of God revealed to us as we are called together into yet this new covenant, bound by love of God and neighbor.

There is yet again a third people called together by the God first seen in the covenant with Israel, continuing in the covenant through Christ with gentiles—and continuing again in the sixth century through the prophet Mohammed. And does the Quran become the face of God to Islam?

We sing a Christian hymn, "There's a Wideness in God's Mercy, like the wideness of the sea." Can this mean that a covenant with creation suggested by its call-and-response mode becomes the ground of subsequent covenants in which the Face of God is discerned, whether dimly or clearly, depending upon the differing needs of the peoples involved? In the freedom of God, it is surely possible. Would we recognize it? Perhaps—if we saw compassion in the ordering of community, even though the way of its exercise differs from our own customary modes.

If there is more than one God-initiated covenant, all subsequent to the primal covenant of creation suggested in Genesis 1 and Psalm 148, then each covenant is validly enacted between God and the covenantal community. Could there be an ultimate goal of a community of covenantal communities? Siblings, not rivals? Delighting in the sharing of the different covenantal calls? Even learning from one another?

Perhaps Psalm 148's hymn of creation has many verses! And perhaps we are called to join in together, letting our own verse add to the contrapuntal harmony of the whole.

POINTS TO PONDER

The universality of Genesis 1 and Psalm 148 should awaken questions of how each religion regards others. Traditionally, it's been relatively easy to assume one's own religion as the standard for all others, or even worse, the replacement of all others. The problem, of course, is that a close scrutiny of one's own religion reveals too many flaws we'd much rather sweep under the proverbial rug. Another "problem" is that once we actually begin to understand other religions, we find not only much to admire, but much that actually looks to us like the praise of God. That is, if "compassion" is a prime quality of God; then the exercise of compassion in creation is also a way of praising God, is it not? When we see ways to ensure that loving compassion is expected civilly as well as individually, aren't we witnessing the universal call through creation being answered with the praise of God, wherever we see it occurring? On what basis would you agree or disagree? Does your own faith community have formal or informal interactions with other faith communities?

The twentieth century pioneered new phases in inter-religious relations. Inter-religious dialogue helped religious people of every tradition to understand those of other traditions. This in turn led to inter-religious cooperation in addressing the suffering in the world. Mutual appreciation among religions, extending kindness to one another, and seeking together to provide compassionate care to alleviate suffering anywhere in the world, is a form of praising God, echoing the togetherness of God's call in Genesis 1, and creation's answer in Psalm 148.

What things could deeper inter-religious cooperation do? We see it already in national and international organizations as people from several religions work together to address suffering in this world, whether because of wars, migrations, persecutions, natural disasters, or pandemics. Name the ways your own congregation, either on its own or in cooperation with others, adopts practices and causes that help our beleagured Earth recover from toxic harms. Can you also name ways your own congregation, either on its own or in cooperation with others, seeks to work with other religious organizations toward identified common goods? Remembering the qualities listed in psalm 146's praise of God, can you name the ways your congregation, either on its own or in cooperation with others, reaches out to alleviate the suffering of the community/ nation/world's "least"? Might working together to heal the planet and tend the "least" be an ultimate form of praising God? Let us praise God together, in our deeds!

CONTEMPORARY PSALM/PRAYER

God our creator, the trees and the hills rise up with us to
   praise your name.
Lowing cows and wild beasts of the forests call us to pause
   and lift our voices.
The rushing wind blows where it will, and we are filled with
   your Spirit of love.
The sun, moon, and stars—our faithful sisters and brothers—
show us your light and keep watch with us.
Even the elements, the rain and the hail, beat out your rhythm
   of praise;
Grant us grace to live in covenant with you and with all you
   have created,
remembering your promise to set free this bountiful Earth
   from bondage.
We wait in eager longing for the time when all creation will
   gather
on your holy mountain and join the song the morning stars
   began.
Open our hearts and bring us together with princes and
   paupers, young and old
strangers and friends, men and women alike to sing and
   shout with joy:
"Behold the wonders of God's creation! Praise for God's everlasting love."
Amen.

～ 21st MEDITATION ～

PSALM 150

Praise the Lord!

Read Psalm 150

THERE ARE precisely twelve lines in this final psalm, eleven of which begin with the word "Praise" and the twelfth of which concludes with the shout, "Praise the Lord!" Previous psalms have spoken of instruments of praise—indeed, the very word "psalter" refers to a harp-like instrument which, along with the lute, the timbrel, and the lyre, are united in melody to praise God.

This one hundred and fiftieth psalm concludes the Book of Psalms with a mighty Hallelujah Chorus, but that chorus is not an end, but a new beginning that continues even unto our own day—it begins an unending chorus sung through years, decades,

centuries, and millennia, pointing yet to its continuation in the
years, decades, centuries, and millennia to come. Praise the Lord!

The concluding doxology in the whole psalter is not simply
this final chapter of twelve lines. Indeed, the doxology is fore-
told in all the psalms, finally coming to its fullest expression in
these last five. Essential in the naming of praise is a description of
the God to whom we give our praise. Remember its summary in
Psalm 146? That listing of divine qualities is not novel; it weaves
its way throughout the whole Scripture. We Christians see it culminating in the revelation of the divine nature in Jesus; Jews see
it culminating in the Torah and the prophets. Muslims see it in
the prophet Mohammed and in the Quran. These are not contra-
dicting revelations, but complementary revelations manifesting
the nature of God for us.

These concluding psalms in the final doxology suggest that
there is a way of praising God that is even fuller than we can convey
in our music, our poetry, our art, and our literature, inspiring and
beautiful as these may be. Rather, the ultimate praise of God is
to reflect the image of God in the way we live, and that image,
again and again in these psalms, is love and compassion. Insofar
as we are compassionate in our personal and political care of the
"least" in our society, we are reflecting the image of God, which is
the praise of God. When we provide ways for the poor to be able
to feed themselves and their families, we are praising God. When
we strive to "set the prisoner free" by helping prisoners to become
contributing members of community when they are released, we
are praising God. When we care for those who face physical challenges in society, we are praising God; when we raise up those
who are bowed down, when we protect strangers and support the
fatherless and the widow, we are praising God. When we strive for
peace, for community, for greater wellbeing, we are praising God.
The prophet Micah said it well: "What does the Lord require of you

but to do justice, to love kindness, and to walk humbly with your God?" Is not this the deepest, truest way of all to show the praise of God? Can we all, all, all finally just be a living hallelujah chorus so that our whole lives are echoes of the primal praise of God, whose steadfast love endures forever, whose faithfulness endures forever, whose compassion endures forever, and most awesomely for Christians, whose highest majesty is in the lowliness of a manger and the forsakenness of a cross, both embraced in resurrection power? Oh, with gratitude and humility, with all our being, let us sing and strive to be the living praise of God!

POINTS TO PONDER

The deepest point to ponder is the connection between the way we live and how we praise our God.

CONTEMPORARY PSALM/PRAYER

God of glory, you breathe life into us,
and we praise you with our every breath.
We come before you with a great and joyous noise, with
    dancing and music.
The hills and trees, the rocks and streams, the sky above us
    join the song.
May our hearts unfold like flowers before you, reflecting the
    light of your glory.
May our tongues sing a thousand praises and tell of your
    marvelous deeds.
May we walk in your steps and praise you with our love for
    one another.
May our glad Hallelujahs welcome the Sun of Righteousness,
rising to heal and set the prisoner free, lifting the poor from

the dust,
and offering life and health and peace to all in honor of your
    name.
Praise the Lord! Amen.

Acknowledgments

My colleague Blair Gilmer Meeks and I worked closely together as I developed the text, and she developed the contemporary psalms/prayers. Her prayers emerged from deeply within her soul in response to the emotional call of each psalm. It was an immense privilege for me to work with such a gifted poet; her prayers became mine as well as we worked together.

Two sources were particularly helpful to me as I worked through these psalms. The first was the 2014 *New Cambridge Bible Commentary on the Psalms*, edited and written by Walter Brueggemann and William H. Bellinger, Jr.

In addition to this invaluable written work, I am intensely grateful to Walter Brueggemann for his helpful responses when I consulted him on particularly troublesome problems the Psalms raised for me. I am indebted to him for his kind and helpful advice.

My second resource was the immensely valuable The Jewish Study Bible, featuring The Jewish Publication Society Tanakh Translation of Torah, Nevi'im, and Kethuvim. This volume is edited by Adele Berlin and Marc Zvi Brettler, with Michael Fishbane as consulting editor. Particularly helpful is the extensive commentary published alongside each Psalm. The copy I used was published by the Oxford University Press in 2004; its original publication was by the Jewish Publication Society in 1985 and again in 1999.

The translation of the Psalms I used was either that included in the Brueggemann/Bellinger commentary, or the New American Standard version of 1989. Occasionally, as noted in the text, I used the King James Version.

As a theologian writing meditations on the Psalms, I am venturing into a field I have not formally studied. Therefore, any egregious errors that might be found in my treatment of the Psalms are, unfortunately, entirely my own.

Made in United States
Orlando, FL
16 February 2024

43751797R00071